Teach Your Child to Read

The Good Parents' Guide to Reading, Writing and Spelling

Peter Young
and Colin Tyre

Fontana/Collins

First published by Fontana Paperbacks,
8 Grafton Street, London W1X 3LA

Set in Linotron Plantin
Made and printed in Great Britain by
William Collins Sons & Co. Ltd, Glasgow

Peter Young and Colin Tyre have both been classroom teachers. They first worked together as joint consultants to the project for the teaching of reading for the National Development Programme for Computer Assisted Learning. More recently they were joint directors of the Department of Education and Science Action Research Project on dyslexic pupils. Colin Tyre is chief education psychologist for the county of South Glamorgan. He was previously county adviser for special education. Peter Young has been a senior local inspector of primary education and tutor at the Cambridge Institute of Education. He was a member of the Warnock Committee and has written a number of books for schools. Their latest publication was *Dyslexia or Illiteracy?*(1983).

Contents

Appendices

Notes

1 Throughout this book we have used the term parents for parents singly, male and female, jointly, natural, adoptive, foster, surrogate, grand and for those known, in the jargon of sociology, as caregivers, both for convenience and in the belief that parenthood, like beauty, is in the eye of the beholders, those darling kids, as Kipling called them, for whom we have written it.

2 We have written throughout on the proper assumption that all parents will have identified and be meeting those special needs of children who have handicaps, disabilities and defects of body, mind or senses, and that they are well able to make such modifications to the programmes we describe to enable their children to enjoy and benefit from them. Their ingenuity, patience and persistence have encouraged us in ours.

3 For the convenience of readers we have written as parents and use, throughout, the parental, unroyal 'we'. We have not wasted words, therefore, in distinguishing which did what in the certain knowledge that readers will not be interested to know and that, should either be challenged, he would say it was the other! On that, as upon all that we have written, happily, we agree.

1

Parents and Literacy

We've written this book to help parents teach their children to read. Fortunately, some children need very little teaching or encouragement. Wendy, at 2 years 11 months, had had no direct help in learning to read when her mother found her sprawled on the floor with a book of fairy tales open in front of her. The book was upsidedown. 'What are you doing?' her mother asked. 'Reading,' Wendy answered. 'With the book upsidedown?' teased her mother. 'Yes,' replied Wendy, 'it's easier upsidedown. Listen!' And, to her mother's amazement, Wendy read aloud with hardly a pause or stumble. Wendy's mother didn't know that research has shown that some children do, in fact, find it easier to read print when it's upsidedown. When we asked her what she had done about Wendy's upsidedown reading, she said, 'Oh, we just weaned her off it!' Which, we reflected, is the sort of thing parents are good at.

Some children, however, need a lot of help. Phil's father told us how he had struggled, with the help of teachers and specialists, to start Phil reading. 'Nothing worked. Then you showed me how to get Phil reading in unison with me. Now, at last, at 13, he can read. If I'd only known how easy it was, I'd have saved Phil years of failure and the family years of misery. But what I've learnt is that the important thing is not *what* you teach, but *how* you teach it. You've got to teach so that kids want to go on reading. I shudder to think how I'd have felt if I'd taught Phil to read and he'd never wanted to open a book again in his life! Phil's real success is that he enjoys reading. It's as if he's got to be reading all the time to catch up on those wasted years.' How to teach so that children want to go on doing things is something else parents are good at.

We want this book to help you teach your child to read early, to read well and to go on reading. Taking an active interest in your child's reading will help enormously. Having fun for five or ten minutes every day teaching children to read, write and spell, in the

11

ways we suggest, will make sure that they progress at their own rate and in their own ways, without pressure and without fear of failure. This is because the methods we have developed over the years working with children, teachers, parents and other researchers are largely modelled on how parents teach and upon a holistic model of reading. By a holistic model we mean one in which the whole activity of reading, writing and spelling is more than the sum of its parts. Just as a pudding is very much more than the sum of its ingredients, so reading, and its related skills of writing and spelling, are very much more than the sum of the bits – the letters, their shapes and sounds, the words and their meanings and spellings. When, some years ago, we first explained to parents that we wanted them to teach their children to read by reading to them and getting their children to read along with them, one mother couldn't wait to try it out, and announced, 'It makes sense. Of course it'll work. That's how we teach them to walk – we walk with them and hold them and then, when they're ready, we let go!' Another parent suggested that it was how we taught children to ride a bike. It was a suggestion we adopted.

Maybe, because we have learnt so much from working with parents, parents find it easier than teachers to adopt our holistic approach to teaching reading. Someone once said that if children had to wait until they went to school to learn to talk, then there would be a lot of mute and speech-defective children and an even greater shortage of speech therapists! It is because parents teach their children to understand and to express themselves in language so successfully that, in a literate society such as ours, they are, in our opinion, the ideal teachers of their own children in the arts and skills of reading, writing and spelling.

Great Expectations

One reason why we parents are such good teachers of our own children is that we are 'expectant'. Not only were we expectant parents but, once our children were born, we went on expecting. We expected them to suckle, smile, gurgle, sit up, stand, walk and talk. Having great expectations is much more than just being hopeful or optimistic. Expectation is so important that scientific experiments are plagued by it and life thrives on it. The more powerful the witchdoctor or the more splendidly credentialled the specialist, the more powerful the medicine. So, in medicine, we have placebos and double-blind tests, in which not even the doctors dispensing the drugs know which are fakes and which drugs are being tested. In social psychology we have the Hawthorne effect: change the working or learning conditions and performance improves. In interpersonal relations, the higher our expectations of people, the better their performance. One mother told us, 'It was only when I started to praise Rex for his reading that I realized how much I'd got into the habit of putting him down, finding fault, expecting him to be clumsy, saying "No" and "Don't". All the time I was expecting him to fail. I used not to be like that. And he was getting worse. Now I've started praising him again, I find I'm on the lookout for things I can say "Yes" and "Good" to. Because I expect him to be better, he's getting better – and not just with his reading and writing!'

One of the important ways in which parents use their expectations of children's progress and development is in keeping a sharp eye open for signs that they may be lagging behind or having difficulties in learning. It is because parents have been recognized by doctors and educators as being so good at identifying, anticipating and meeting their children's needs that, increasingly, parents are being welcomed as full partners in the education of their children. Parental participation, as school governors, as members of the multidisciplinary team to assess special educational needs, as partners in the teaching of mathematics and reading, has become an accepted and vital contribution to the educational process. This book extends the concept of parents as active partners. It helps parents to base the education of their children upon achieving the highest possible levels of literacy.

Teaching our children to read, write and spell is fun. And it is giving them a jump-start in the educational process. For the proof of the pudding described in this book is when our children are not only reading for enjoyment, but when they are able to learn by reading. It is in this respect that the scope of the book is from language to literacy, and from literacy to learning across the curriculum. In short, literacy for living.

Why Parents?

In 1967 the Plowden Report on primary education in England and Wales maintained that 'by involving the parents, the children may be helped'. It reported research it had commissioned that demonstrated that the most significant factor in determining levels of children's academic achievement was parental interest in their education. The Warnock Report, 'Special Educational Needs', 1978, recommended better working relations between professionals and parents as partners. It urged that parents should be involved in decisions about their children's special educational needs, and that they be listened to as the best indicators, in many cases, of those needs. It recommended that, 'In the earliest years parents rather than teachers should be regarded, wherever possible, as the main educators of their children'.

Of particular interest to us, so far as reading is concerned, is the report of the Bullock Committee, 'A Language for Life', 1975, which commended schools that involved parents in helping children learn to read. 'The best way to prepare the very young child for reading,' it suggested, 'is to hold him in your lap and read aloud to him stories he likes, over and over again.' The Report also observed that 'There are many well attested cases of parents who have been highly successful in helping their children to learn to read'. But the Report stopped short of making a straight recommendation that parents should teach their children to read.

At that time there were very good reasons for this. Schools had been established to produce a literate population at a time when most of the population was illiterate. As recently as the 1872 Education Act which made education compulsory and universally available in England and Wales, over a quarter of the adult population was illiterate. Prior to that time most children were taught to read by their parents, like Samuel Johnson who learned to read by the age of 3. But, with the setting up of schools, the myth has gradually been perpetuated that school is the *only* place in which one learns to read. At one time, schools were divided into two camps: those who believed that reading should be taught by the 'look and say' method, and those who held it should be taught by the 'phonic' method. The 'look and say' method relied on using flash cards and reading books which repeated words over and over until the children recognized them. This resulted in some very odd language in the early primers:

14

Oh, oh! Look, look!
Look. See the ball.
Look, the ball!

The phonic method concentrated on the sounds of letters and on 'building up' words. The early primers regaled children with text such as 'The mat sat on the cat' or 'Dan the tan man ran to the can in the caravan'! Today, many teachers still believe that it should be taught by a modification of one or both of these methods. But, as the Bullock Report pointed out, 'Too much attention has been given to polarized opinions about approaches to the teaching of reading. . . . The most effective teaching of reading is that which gives the pupil the various skills he needs to make the fullest possible use of context cues in the search for meaning.' Today it is possible to use methods, which are simple and effective, which *do* ensure that children get meaning from print right from the start. The holistic approach, which we have developed with parents of young children and with parents of older pupils with extreme difficulties in learning to read, makes it possible for parents to be 'the main educators of their children' in reading, writing and spelling in the early years, and to continue as partners throughout their children's education.

Why Teach Reading?

Reading is enjoyable, informative, useful and, in our culture, essential. For children it's magic. The sudden realization that they are reading hits some children with all the force of a 'Eureka!' experience. When our children have learned to read, we, as parents, are both proud for them and relieved that they have achieved this milestone in their development. When our children fail to read and fail to respond to teachers' specialist help, we suspect their eyesight, their hearing, their mental abilities, their heredity, ourselves and the way we have brought them up. Of all the hundreds of things we may want our children to achieve, socially, athletically, musically, intellectually, or in any other way, reading is an achievement which looms large in our hopes. A mother of an 11-year-old boy, who was clearly talented in mathematics, expressed her frustration, 'Because he can't read, Ian's more handicapped than if he were blind. Until he can read he will never be able to realize his mathematical abilities.'

Reading, it was once suggested, will become less important in the 'electronic global village' into which our children are growing. Nothing could be further from the truth. It is as silly a misreading of what is happening as the belief that pocket calculators and computers would make a knowledge of computation and mathematics less important. As we have already seen in the past two decades, these developments have simply accelerated the demands for higher levels of numeracy and literacy. Unfortunately, the signs abound that not only are we failing to keep up with demands, we are falling further behind. This would not be our concern here if we believed that the position was understood, being acted upon and likely to be put right. We would not like to *sound* alarmist. We are alarmed. But we allow ourselves that luxury only because we are proposing a solution. Here are some of the facts. First we need to put them in perspective.

In his fascinating study, *Literacy and Development in the West*, Carlo Cipolla pointed out as long ago as 1969 that, 'In an advanced industrial society a person with less than ten or twelve years of schooling is functionally illiterate. New and advanced technologies have altered the proportions of things. . . . Under these conditions, the best solutions are those which inherently contain a high degree of flexibility and adaptability to change.' But, as the Bullock Report acknowledged in connection with the ability to read with understanding and insight, 'Research strongly suggests that as many as one third of the population may be incompetent'. Functional literacy, a UNESCO concept, means having the reading skills in order to function effectively in all those activities in which literacy is needed in a society. In England, for instance, six adults in every hundred, about two million people, are functionally illiterate.

It is against this background that we need to look at what is going on in our schools. Dr Vera Southgate, investigating what teachers were doing to extend the reading abilities of 7- to 8-year-olds, found that the children were getting no more than an average of thirty seconds' individual help at a time. What they needed at this important stage in their education, she considered, were longer periods of individual help for, say, fifteen to twenty minutes. In Scotland, James Maxwell's study, sponsored by the Scottish Education Department, found that functional literacy was not taught, that inadequate attention was given to matching pupils' reading abilities to

16

their text books across the curriculum in secondary schools, and that 'over half of the good readers and three-quarters of the poor readers failed to make any progress in their reading status' from 12 years of age onwards.

More recently, the Thomas Report, 'Improving Primary Schools', 1985, made known its findings in and recommendations for London schools. It agreed with those parents who believe primary schools expect too little of their pupils. 'Too often new work was at much the same level of difficulty as the old,' the Report says. There was a need for greater concern for quality rather than quantity, and for higher expectations of children. Underexpectation took two forms: an over-concentration upon the three Rs and too narrow a curriculum. 'Achievements were being earned at too high a price in relation to the rest of the curriculum and to the detriment of the children. Reading, writing and mental arithmetic were better learnt in use.' In other schools, underexpectation took the form of providing 'a wide-ranging but undemanding curriculum'. In language work, teachers underestimated the language powers of working-class children. In reading there was evidence that, despite the 17 principal recommendations and 333 conclusions and recommendations of the Bullock Report, which, ten years earlier, covered every aspect of the teaching of reading and the other uses of English in schools, there was a need for increased attention to linking reading and writing skills to direct experience and to using contextual cues to meaning. The value of literature as a source of pleasure and excitement and as a model for children's writing style, as well as a means of improving their reading abilities, was stressed. The Report recommended that more attention should be given to teaching children how to use books for finding out information and how to vary their reading styles according to circumstances. Handwriting was a skill which needed more specific and careful teaching whilst, 'Spelling and grammar require development in the context of conveying meaning. They are not best tackled in isolation. Children should have many opportunities for writing for real purposes and to many different audiences.'

Her Majesty's Inspectors in their annual expenditure survey, published in May 1985, showed that children's education is being seriously affected by the 'deteriorating quality and appropriateness' of the educational environment, by dilapidated school buildings, inadequate resources and outdated text books. The Thomas Report on London primary education, like so many reports these days, recommends the involvement of parents in the teaching of reading and stresses that no child should be prevented from taking books home from school. In this context it is sad to find that Her Majesty's Inspectors in Wales have found that some schools receive more money from parents than from local authorities for books and other educational supplies. As equipment wears out, schools are having increasing difficulty in replacing it and 'pupils' learning experiences are impoverished as a result'. In our view it is not the function of parents to counteract poor teaching and augment inadequate supplies of books and equipment. But it is our role as parents to make sure that we do all in our power to develop the abilities and skills of our children to the limit of their potential, so that they may derive the maximum benefit from their education.

One effect of the narrowness of so many school curricula, with their preoccupation with the three Rs, was revealed in the recent survey by the National Foundation for Educational Research which showed that 40 per cent of teachers of 9- to 11-year-olds taught science less than once a week. Yet, according to Sir George Porter, FRS, director of the Royal Institution and president of the Association for Science Education, ignorance of natural science was 'close to being a national disaster'. He warned that two nations were growing up, those who understood the modern world and those who were 'mentally deficient in that their minds were not connected to the mainstream of thought and activity of mankind'. However, had Sir George Porter examined the situation in music, the arts, history or geography, he would have found a very similar imbalance in the curricula of many schools. In the nation's primary schools there have never been enough qualified teachers of music and, were it not for the Schools Service of the BBC, very many schools would provide no musical education whatsoever. We mention this because we have found from experience that often the hallmark of a good school is that its music flourishes, chorally and instrumentally. If the head and staff can get the music right, the chances are that they have got everything else right. Invariably, too, such schools have long enjoyed close cooperation with parents, essential in the development of musical abilities!

Clearly, if parents can play a part in helping their children to learn to read, write and spell, then the better they do so, the greater the advantage both to their children and to the schools and teachers responsible for their education. In this respect, before we turn to look more closely at parents, schools and reading, a significant indication of the importance of parental influence on their children's academic achievement emerged from the report of Lord Swann's Committee on the education of ethnic minority children. One of the factors the Committee investigated was the extent to which parents helped their children with homework and study for examinations. Whereas 60 per cent of white children said their parents helped them, only 44 per cent of West Indian parents helped, compared with 70 per cent of Pakistani and Bangladeshi children. As one would expect, the Asian children achieved considerably better O level passes than the West Indian children. These, of course, are generalized figures. We are reminded of the West Indian pupil at a summer holiday school we had organized to help immigrant school leavers improve their language skills. Asked if he had a job to go to he replied, 'I'm just a voluntary worker here at the summer school. Next term I'm going to Cambridge to read biochemistry' – which was not what we had expected! We can be sure *his* parents had taken an active interest in his reading, studies and homework.

Carlo Cipolla, whom we quoted earlier, concludes his study of literacy in the West by pointing to the very defects in our educational system with which we have been concerned.

In a highly dynamic industrial environment, an educational institution, no matter how excellent, is bound to become rapidly obsolete if it is hampered by traditionalism and if its change is dependent upon complicated and time-consuming bureaucratic procedures. Ultimately the effectiveness of an institution depends upon the quality of its members and of their leaders, but there is no doubt that rigid institutional arrangements can frustrate and obliterate a generous amount of good will and human energy.

We believe that parents are able to provide 'a generous amount of good will and human energy' which can overcome many of the deficiencies of our educational system. They have always done so and we hope this book will help them to do even more with enjoyment and without stress.

Parents, Schools and Reading

Although the Bullock Committee could report that 'children with a mental age of four and a half to five can quite happily learn to read . . . and there is ample evidence of children learning to read at home well before reaching even this kind of mental age', it did no more than recommend that parents had an important part to play 'in preparing the child for the early stages of reading'. Until recently, this has been the received wisdom in most schools. When we asked parents what their experience had been when they approached schools and asked how they might help their children to read, a clear picture emerged of 'hands off'.

WHAT SCHOOLS TOLD PARENTS WHO WANTED TO HELP THEIR
   CHILDREN TO READ

* Don't interfere – you could easily confuse your child.
* Leave it to the teachers – there's plenty of time.
* Methods have changed since you were at school – we have a special scheme and special equipment.
* Don't worry – you'll make your child overanxious.
* Parents are too emotionally involved to teach their own children.
* You'll only put pressure on the child – when children are ready, they'll read.

From some schools parents still get advice like this. One mother was told, as soon as she uttered the word 'reading', 'Oh, when he's finished his language programme, he'll start on the pre-reading scheme – then he'll start learning to read.' The mother explained that she didn't want to interfere with their programme but, as Jamie could already read, couldn't she let him carry on reading at home!

In contrast, when we ask parents if they would like to help their children learn to read, the answer almost invariably is, 'When can we start?' They are eager to help and if for any reason, such as sickness in the family, they can't, they are keen that someone should act as a substitute for them. What always surprises them is that someone involved in education should be enlisting their help.

In the many areas where schools have invited parents to take part in programmes to help their children learn to read, there has been a similar response from parents. In recent years in London, Haringey, Derbyshire, Huddersfield, Halifax, Leeds, Sheffield, Walsall, Gwent, Mid and South Glamorgan, for instance, there have been well documented projects which have successfully involved parents of children between the ages of 6 to 13 years. In virtually all cases the children made marked progress.

Undoubtedly, the ideal situation for children of school age is when parents and teachers work closely in harmony with one another as equal partners to help children learn to read. The difficulty is that often, when this cooperation is initiated, it may be a case of too little, too late and, in our experience, the help may be neither well conceived nor well implemented. Often it is the delay, rather than parental anxiety or 'interference', which has caused many children to fail to learn to read and to develop learning difficulties. The DES published Her Majesty's Inspectors' discussion document, 'English from 5 to 16', 1984, on 'the key subject in the school curriculum', which made this vital point:

If a basic level of literacy and articulateness is not attained by the age of 7, it becomes very difficult to achieve competence in other learning, much of which relies on the ability to read, to discuss, and to record in writing. The effects may persist, and become increasingly disadvantageous, throughout the primary stage and beyond. It is often the case that children of normal intelligence who have reading difficulties at the end of the primary phase are seriously under-achieving at 16.

Unfortunately, if children are to achieve the levels suggested by HMI by 7 years of age, this is going to make considerable demands on many of their teachers. As the document acknowledges, the childrendiffer considerably in their pre-school experience in that 'some will have had books read to them and may have begun to read, whileothers will not'. But the objectives set are not unrealistic or very demanding for 7-year-olds:

Reading
Read and understand labels, simple notices and written instructions

Read with understanding simple stories, rhymes and passages of information, to themselves and aloud

Know the alphabet, and apply their knowledge of alphabetical

21

order when consulting simple dictionaries and other reference books

Have sufficient fluency and motivation to become engrossed in books because of the interest and enjoyment they derive from them

Use books as sources of information to support aspects of their work in the classroom

For a child who has begun to read before starting school, there is a reasonable chance that these objectives may be reached by 7 years of age. But, as many parents know from their own experience, some children have reached these levels of attainment by 5 or 6 years of age, whilst others of average ability are still struggling to reach them at 11 and 12. It is not simply that children differ from one another. What makes the difference is the quality of stimulation, encouragement and experience with books and with reading which children get at home with their parents, family and friends.

What is needed is that all parents who can read themselves should help their children to learn to read, write and spell and should go on taking an active interest in their children's reading and study habits throughout their school lives. Even when young people get to university, to our certain knowledge, it is perfectly possible that they have received no adequate training in studying and in the use of books. *If parents are to give children help and support, then they may need simple guidelines. But what we have found is that the guidelines they require are, in very large measure, reassurance that what they are doing and what they want to go on doing, is usually right. While developing our own experimental designs and models we found that the more we responded to the children's needs and abilities, the more these designs resembled what successful parents were already doing and had been doing for centuries.*

The model for reading and for the teaching of reading we have perfected began in neuropsychology and information theory, but has ended up back in the parents' lap. What parents have done instinctively in responding to their children's curiosity and prompting has proved, once more, to be the best model. It is another case of rediscovering the virtues of mothers' milk.

As we show in detail in the later chapters, how we play and talk with our children can lead naturally into talking them into reading. We show how, from an understanding of reading as a way of getting meaning from print, parents can progress from reading *to* their children to reading *with* them. In turn, this shared and paired reading, or reading in unison, leads on, step by step, to independent reading and to study skills, to learning by reading.

Similarly, talking about what our children have drawn or painted leads naturally to writing down what they have said. By writing over, tracing and copying, children are introduced to making letter shapes and to writing and spelling. We demonstrate how parents can help their children to progress from learning to write their own names to learning to read, write and spell and develop these skills, hand in hand, until they achieve efficient study habits across all the subjects of the school curriculum. Throughout, our emphasis is on simple and practical ways in which parents can help their children to learn through games and activities and ensure that success builds upon success.

Before getting down to the programme, therefore, we need first to identify just why and how parents are such successful teachers.

2

What Parents do Best

Becoming a parent is the most creative act anyone can perform. But, because parenthood can happen to almost anyone, it is taken very much for granted by everyone else except the parents themselves who, depending upon their circumstances, regard it as miraculous or cataclysmic. Overwhelmed by awe, anxiety, fear and wonder, feeling fraught and frail, we suddenly find ourselves surrounded by experts. It is a moment when even pregnant gynaeocologists, paediatricians and midwives are subject to role reversal and, surrounded by experts, have been known to feel vulnerable as they themselves are elevated to parenthood. But parenthood is not just a moment, but a process of becoming and of hanging in for decades, and it is that which makes it truly creative and beyond the discoveries of science or the inventions of art. Not that the experts would ever let us think it so. When our children start school, whether we are doctors, educators, psychiatrists or peasants, we all sit humbly at the feet of teachers who set out the shortcomings of the monsters with whom we have plagued them – or, very occasionally, the achievements of the darlings we have delivered to delight them – and heaven help us if we interfere. All the experts, of course, depend for their livelihoods on our productive capacity as parents. They have, therefore, a vested interest in making us feel superfluous and themselves indispensable! It is time that, as parents, we took this fresh look at ourselves and all the things we do achieve with our children in the pre-school years. Perhaps, after all, there are some things in which parents are the experts.

Home is Best

In the jargon of education, the area in which parents excel is in providing 'a learning environment'. A learning environment is simply one which makes learning possible. The child who is hungry is too distracted to want to learn, he wants food. The cold child is an incurious child who wants warmth and shelter. Parents provide for all of these basic needs and for much more without which there would be neither survival nor learning.

By the age of 5 years, parents have virtually taught their children to be independent. It is an incredible achievement.

WHAT PARENTS TRADITIONALLY TEACH IN 60 MONTHS

* Crawling, standing, walking, running, jumping, climbing and going up and down stairs.
* Eating using knife, fork and spoon.
* Drinking from cup or glass.
* Dressing, tying knots, use of buttons and zips.
* Washing, bathing, cleaning teeth.
* Toilet training by day and night.
* Skipping, hopping, skating and cycling (but not 'traffic safe').
* Swimming, in learner pool.
* Playing alone, with other children and adults, taking turns and learning the rules.
* To know own name, sex, age, birthday, address and way around neighbourhood (not 'traffic safe').
* To use pencils, crayons, paints to draw people, houses, common objects; circles, squares, lines, triangles (but not a diamond).
* To count to about 20, know fingers on each hand ($5+5=10$), recognize digits, repeat numbers like 47582.
* To cut out common shapes with scissors, cut things in halves, make models of things in 3D.
* To behave appropriately with family, relatives, friends, strangers in a variety of social settings.
* To talk and to understand language, using complete grammatical system correctly; to ask and answer questions; to follow and to give instructions; to follow and to tell stories; to describe, compare and contrast; to define things by their use; to know names of days, months, seasons, colours, coins; to use language in social relationships and to guide actions; to use about 2000 words.
* To enjoy being read to and to have begun to read – some to read fluently, some only recognizing odd words and letters.

* To write own name and most letters of alphabet – some to write messages, some to enjoy copying.
* To care for younger children, for pets, performing useful tasks about the house and garden with minimum of supervision.

Thanks to their parents' teaching, by 5 years of age children are very competent and socialized people. In agricultural communities, they can perform a variety of useful tasks. In industrial countries, 150 years ago, they were working in mills at 6 and 7, learning to tend machines by 'sitting next to Nellie'. Today, in the Third World, children of 6 are active contributors to their families' survival. In our literate societies, parents who expected their children to walk and to talk expect them to learn to read. If the children can read already by the age of 5, they are off to an excellent start and the chances are that their parents taught and encouraged them. If they can't read, then the chances are that their parents have held back from teaching them in the fear that this was a skill best taught by 'experts', the teachers in school. Now parents rightly expect that children will quickly learn to read in their first year at school. The foundations they laid in the development of their children's language should guarantee this. It is in the early teaching of language that parents excel.

Babies are Born Teachers

What makes it possible for children to learn so much is that they are born teachers. They survive by exchanging a physical for a psychological umbilical cord. They teach their parents to attach themselves to them. Their hunger cries demand that we feed them, their distress cries alert us to change their nappies, their gurgles set us off talking to them, their eyes hold our attention, their warm vulnerability makes us pick them up and their smiles reward us. Whether or not babies are imprinted by their parents or other adults to whom they attach themselves is not known, but there's no doubt that they do imprint themselves on us. For, as parents, real or substitute, we are programmed to respond to them and to secure their survival. Babies are organisms programmed to trigger the parenting behaviours latent in us and we find that we, too, are their born teachers.

Parents are Born Teachers

Sexual reproduction in homo sapiens is far more subtle and complex than the elementary gymnastics of sex manuals. The successful selection and courtship of mates is designed to provide mothers with protection during the vulnerable days of pregnancy and delivery, and for the survival and upbringing of the offspring during infancy. The procreative drive is no more satisfied by the birth of the child than it was by orgasm. Survival of the species demands that the drive is only satisfied when the child attains physical, social and intellectual maturity and independence. Babies have been given a two-shot genetic endowment from the species' gene pool which ensures they are each unique. To realize their uniqueness and their full potential, they must be taught by their parents. Babies are born learners, programmed to survive by observing, exploring and thinking. They form hunches or hypotheses based on their perceptions of their surroundings, and they test them out. Having taught us to attach ourselves to them, they are quick to establish an interactive relationship. They want to learn. We want to teach them. We must catch the moment.

The baby-parent system is not a closed, but an open one. The basic survival programme is developed and orchestrated to equip the child with the traditions and behaviours appropriate to its community, society and culture. Nowhere is this more in evidence than in the way in which children learn and parents teach language. This is where parents excel. Because learning to read is part of learning language, we need to look at what parents do to teach language in greater detail. As Julian Huxley put it, 'Man added tradition to heredity'.

LADs and LASSes

Children are born linguists. They have a natural ability to learn their mother tongue, any mother tongue. They learn it partly by imitation, partly by invention and largely by social interaction with their parents. Alone, at 5 months, they may be overheard babbling quietly to themselves so convincingly that we may think there is someone with them carrying on a conversation. By 12 months they may have said their first words and show signs of understanding simple instructions. From the first words progress is usually bewilderingly fast. One mother exclaimed, 'He's only just started to talk – now I'm having to feed him a word a minute!' Another told her 25-month-old daughter not to argue, only to be told, 'If you arg me, I'll arg you!'

The capacity of children to acquire language has suggested to Naom Chomsky, the famous linguistician of Massachusetts Institute of Technology, that they have a Language Acquisition Device – a LAD. It not merely enables them to acquire vocabulary and syntax or grammar, but also to invent and order words for themselves. The 2-year-old who announces, 'I seed three mouses' is generating language according to rules he has discovered for himself. Wisely, his mother will not tell him he has made a mistake or say she cannot understand, but may well say, 'Oh, you saw three mice, did you.' Her reply not only shows that she understood and keeps the conversation moving forward, it also provides a model of correct usage. It is this sort of interaction which Jerome Bruner typifies as the parents' role in providing what he calls a Language Acquisition Support System, a LASS. Parents and children want to communicate and language will make communication so much easier. So keeping the transaction going backwards and forwards, bouncing it from one to the other, is what the language game is all about.

The language game is played in real situations which, for the most part, are the shared activities and experiences of parent and child. Most of the time they are talking about themselves and what they are doing and experiencing. Parents act as word banks, memory banks and word processors. They name objects and the child learns there is a name for each thing and each thing has a name. The children think and ask questions which enable them to clothe their thoughts in words. They classify, and their parents' answers help them to sort dogs into animals and cats from dogs, and lions and tigers into cats which are also animals. They learn to ask and answer questions, explain, relate, compare, contrast, narrate and describe. Everything is in a social setting and they are not just learning language, but how to organize their world, how to behave and how people relate to and interact with one another. They are learning not the vocabulary and grammar of a dead language, but language as a living part of their own cultural and traditional inheritance.

When Professor Barbara Tizard of London University studied tapes of parent-child conversations at home, she found that parents were averaging twenty-seven conversations an hour. These exchanges between pre-school children and their busy parents, during the everyday activities of meals, cooking, cleaning, washing, playing and shopping, fed the children's insatiable curiosity and lively intellects. In real-life situations they were playing the language game and being introduced to 'the three Rs' in a way which was relevant and rewarding and in harmony with their developing and changing understanding. When Barbara Tizard studied tapes of the same children after a year in nursery school, she found that the teachers were only averaging ten conversational exchanges an hour. In contrast with what she calls 'the rich curriculum of the home', the children's opportunities for learning were neither so relevant nor so varied.

What parents and children do naturally, in real and significant everyday situations, helps the children to learn. The parents are not instructing or inculcating, but interacting in a way which facilitates learning. It is in that sense that they are truly teaching.

Lap Learning

Learning at home, however, is more than just the everyday transactions we have described so far. The songs and jingles, nursery rhymes, stories, tongue-twisters, riddles, jokes and half-remembered pop songs or ballads with which we entertain our children are familiarizing them with the warp and weft of language and culture. We feed their imaginations and provide new models and reference points. Words rhyme, play tricks, have rhythms, follow patterns and weave tales of good and bad, courage and cowardice, honesty and deceit, love and hate, near and far, the ordinariness of the strange and the strangeness of the ordinary. We can set off on voyages of discovery naming the parts of our bodies, the Norse and Roman names of our days and months, the Anglo-Saxon names of our domestic animals and the Norman-French names for their meat on our tables. The information doesn't come coded like this, but comes when they want it and in a way which fills them with wonder.

Gradually the flood of 'What is it?' questions is replaced with 'Where?', 'When?', 'Which?' and 'How?' questions and, most demanding of all, 'Why?' questions. Their formulation and answers require increasingly complex grammatical structures. By 3 years of age most children have not only become fluent in the use of all the grammatical structures, but their thinking has become organized and structured too. Events have causes and effects, purposes have reasons, and decisions involve weighing up the values we hold. The children will have become socially adjusted and more amenable, they will have developed in self-awareness and awareness of others, and they will have developed self-esteem. The parents' LASS will have fed the child's LAD with meaning.

Instruction Leads Development

One important characteristic of parental teaching is that it usually precedes development and runs a little bit ahead of the expected next step. We talk to our children before they can talk to us, dandle them before they can stand, walk them before they can walk. Because of the intimacy of the interaction with our children, we are uniquely placed to anticipate and predict what children cannot do, can sometimes do and will next be able to do. Thus, we not only anticipate, but pace their instruction so that the children are also anticipating and developing part-skills in preparation for accomplishment. This is perfectly clear in the way in which we help children to pull themselves up before they can stand erect, and encourage them to take their first supported steps before they can walk.

Of course, in all these cases, the parent has a plan of the step-by-step sequence by which the child is assured of success. As one father told us, 'You build your child up by breaking skills down.' The fact that it works encourages us to go on and apply the same approach to new skills. The children encourage us, too. Their delight is one reward but, perhaps more than that, it is their persistence and perseveration. Watch any child around the age of 12 months who has just learned that she can pick things up between finger and thumb. Pencils, toys, keys, food, the pages of books and papers all have to be picked up and put down again. When we commented on 1-year-old Giles who was carefully opening cupboard doors by turning the small brass keys between finger and thumb, his grandmother added, quite rightly, 'And now he's got that off, you see, he'll be talking next!'

Parents as Teachers

In our experience, most parents regard teaching as a special acquired skill which, like education, only goes on in schools and universities. They imagine words such as caring, instructing and training are likely to be the best ones used to describe what they do. This is much more often the view of British parents than of American or European parents. In Britain, education means something different from training or instruction. Education is thought to have nothing to do with work and vocation. As Sir Alistair Pilkington said, in 1984, in his address to the British Association for the Advancement of Science:

> We make an artificial separation between education and training. This goes right back in history to the monasteries and the guilds, as far back as the 14th century, in fact. Education consisted mainly in Latin, Reading, Writing – the 3 Rs. The guilds looked after training. This country holds on to this separation more tightly than other countries and this is particularly damaging to those whose talents are not recognized by exams.

In fact, education and training are interchangeable synonyms, and to try to separate them and distinguish between them is both misleading and damaging. The same can be said of the terms teaching and instructing. Jerome Bruner quite properly called his important contribution to education, *Towards a Theory of Instruction*.

By education, training or instruction we mean that there is conscious selection of what is to be taught, an attempt to teach it in a way which is appropriate to the abilities and needs of the learner, and that what is taught will be of value. The process of education has been described, therefore, as the mediation and facilitation of learning. Martin Buber, the philosopher, described education as the funnel not the pump. What is important about educational or instructional processes is not so much the actions of the teachers as the learning of the pupils. Without learning there is no education.

Our view is that parents teach and educate their children in the fullest sense of those terms. So important is the part played by parents that geneticists, doctors and psychologists have been carefully studying the relationship between the size of families and the spacing of the children's ages and their intellectual development. Studies have been made in Britain, the United States, France and the Netherlands. All point to a relation between intellectual growth and the size and spacing of the ages in families. The geneticist Theodosius Dobzhansky found what he terms an 'undesirable' relationship between the number of years of schooling mothers have had and the size of their families. Mothers with only a few years of education had twice as many children as mothers with college educations. Many studies confirm that children's scores of academic performance decline with increasing family size. The first-born were usually the most able scholastically; the last-born, in large families, the least able.

The American Association for the Advancement of Science awarded a prize to Robert Zajonc, a psychologist at the University of Michigan, for his work in developing a theory to account for this. Zajonc showed that the intellectual growth of children is influenced by the amount of meaningful interaction between them and their parents. The intellectual input, that is, the use of language intended to help the child to understand, order, classify, manipulate and extend her or his comprehensible world, is usually greater when there are two adults and one infant than when, say, there is one parent and five children all under 7 years of age. Observe a small family talking over their meal, discussing what each has been doing or merely commenting on the names of the food they are eating. Compare that input with what a single parent could possibly talk about or discuss when attempting to feed five hungry infants all clamouring for attention. However, Zajonc showed that the decline of input – and of ability – could be compensated for if children were spaced a few years apart, for then the input from the older children helped the younger ones. Zajonc observed, too, that the decline in intellectual input per child can be counterbalanced in large families if the parents make a deliberate attempt to spend time with each child. He also made the important point that higher intellectual abilities enjoyed by children in small families were gained at a price: children in larger families are more likely to develop social skills, a sense of greater responsibility for others and have more rugged and stable personalities.

If home is such a good place as 'a learning environment', if parents provide such a rich curriculum and if parents are such able teachers from whom their children learn so rapidly, it is time more parents did more to teach their children to read. We hope that what we have said so far will have reassured those who already teach their children and will encourage many more to make a start.

And we don't mean *help* their children, we do mean *teach* them to read. What we have found many parents need is not just encouragement to do more, they need a model of teaching which is rugged and rigorous enough to stand up to the heat and bustle of a busy home. The model of teaching we have found most parents really grab is that of teaching a child to ride a bike. If we've not yet done it, we all know precisely how to go about it.

Learning to Ride a Bike and to Read

At least one doesn't have to have graduated in cycling before one can teach it. This is, perhaps, just as well. A physicist, asked to explain the physics involved in cycling, worked on the problem for a few weeks and came to the conclusion that it was physically impossible!

HOW TO TEACH JACK OR JILL TO RIDE A BIKE

* Make sure they have seen lots of kids cycling.
* Make sure they are bursting to ride themselves.
* Make sure they have pedalled their legs off on a trike.
* Get a bike that's the right size for them to sit on with their feet just touching the ground.
* Sit them on the bike with hands on handlebars, feet on pedals, while you hold them and it securely.
* Trot around with them on the bike still supporting it securely.
* Praise them for steering, pedalling, staying on, balancing, being brave or whatever else you can think of to praise.
* When they are accustomed to being on the bike, release them for a brief moment to run unsupported.
* Make a big production number about their first moment of unsupported riding.
* Continue until the unsupported moments get longer and longer but always stay ready to support. Continue to praise, too.
* Once a child is securely bike-borne, stay around until you are satisfied that the child is competent.
* Support the child during starting and stopping until these are performed safely.

* Limit cycling to a safe area in which supervision is possible before supervised cycling on a safe road.
* Teach the safety code and supervise cycling on roads.

This model of teaching children to ride a bike is precisely what, with minor variations such as the fitting of stabilizers, all parents do. It is also, in its essentials, precisely what parents do when they teach their children language. The children have reached a stage at which they want to talk, they have heard a lot of people talking, their parents support and encourage them. All we are suggesting is that this same model can be applied and, in its essentials, is applied by parents when they teach their children to read.

Much of what parents have already done in language teaching, and in what we have called lap learning, has prepared the way for the next steps. Children often say, when they have learned a new skill, such as cycling, that they have got the knack. We may well say they have got it all together. With their parents' support system, learning to read is just a question of getting the knack and getting it all together. It is another way in which, in the long apprenticeship of childhood, 'parents create persons'. Just as parents have given their children the key to language, so they can give them the key to literacy. If we have a clear picture of all that reading is we shall be better able to teach them to enjoy reading and to learn by reading.

3

Apprenticeship to Reading

Reading words or music, the time or timetables, the signs of weather or of the seasons – reading is simply getting meaning from signs. Reading means meaning. And, just as parents teach their children a little bit ahead of their development, walking them before they can walk, talking with them before they can talk, so they begin teaching reading before they are able to read. In some cases parents carry their children with them so far along this road of apprenticeship to reading that they start reading without any formal instructions at all and never look back. Most of the success which teachers have in schools in starting children off as readers has more to do with the apprenticeship the children have served at home under their parents than with the activities of school or the skills and training of the teachers.

'George is only ten days past his second birthday,' one mother told us, 'and he's just hooked on this book about a man who's always buying clocks. George makes me read it over and over again to him and plays hell if I leave out a single word!' She told us she couldn't wait for George to start reading on his own. We suggested that he might be ready to make a start by reading in unison with her. A week later she told us, 'It worked better than I'd hoped. George loved it. Now we're reading together – and we're off the clock book!' George is just typical of countless numbers of children. He was lucky to have a good mother who walked with him, talked with him and read with him – and George just learned to walk, talk and read. There are so many things which parents do with their children which can start them on the way to reading that it is helpful to examine them.

WHAT PARENTS DO WHICH MAKES LEARNING TO READ EASY

* Encourage attentive listening to instructions, conversation, stories, etc.
* Teach their children to use language for communication.
* Enable their children to think in language.
* Encourage their children to say and sing rhymes, jingles, songs, jokes, riddles, etc.
* Encourage their children to look at things, distinguish between things, classify and talk about them.
* Look at pictures and picture books with their children and talk about them together.
* Encourage their children to draw, paint and model things and to talk about what they have done.
* Read aloud to their children from books, comics, etc.
* Read aloud to others letters, messages, newspapers, books, TV programmes, etc.
* Read silently and act upon what they have read, for example, find and dial a phone number, use instructions such as recipes, manuals, etc.
* Read silently for their own enjoyment and become absorbed in newspaper or book.
* Use common signs in home, street, on TV etc. and comment on them, for example 'Oh, there's the parking sign!' 'Oops – there's that red light again!' etc.
* Encourage children to write own name.
* Encourage children to look at books and to 'read' them.

Although these activities are still a long way from actually reading, they contain three vital ingredients with which children must be familiar if they are to learn to read.

THREE VITAL INGREDIENTS PARENTS TEACH ABOUT READING

1. Reading gives information and enjoyment.
2. Reading may be silent, aloud or result in direct action.
3. Reading uses language in more precise and complex ways than spoken language.

Reading for Information and Enjoyment

By reading to, and in front of, children they learn both the purposes and pleasures of print. At the same time, they come to realize that reading is a skill which has status. Finally, just as children have been helped to learn to walk, talk or cycle by seeing their parents and others perform these activities efficiently, so they have been given a model of effective and efficient reading. The model of reading as a pleasurable, useful and worthwhile activity practised by parents or brothers and sisters in the home is enough to encourage most children to want to make it their own. In homes where parents are illiterate or make very little use of print in any shape or form, it helps children enormously if they know that their parents nevertheless value the act of reading and admire those who can read. Clearly, the better the model of reading provided by the parents, the more highly the children will regard it.

With our children's best interests at heart, therefore, no matter how highly or lightly we regard reading, we should always endeavour to talk about it positively and accord it, and those who use it, a high status. Parents who claim that their children's difficulties in reading are 'just like his father's' or 'hereditary – she must have got it from the mother-in-law' are making things worse. They are lowering expectations of success and raising the spectre of failure. The hard genetic evidence that reading difficulties are inherited, like eye colour or attached ear lobes, is very slight, hard to find, and harder still to prove. What we do know is that we are *all* descended from illiterate ancestors. Given reasonable vision, hearing and speech, all our ancestors needed to become literate was the motivation and the opportunity. Literacy, like language, is environmentally determined. As parents, we must provide the right motivation, the right opportunities and the right environment in which reading is an enjoyable and useful activity.

Reading to our children, reading for our own enjoyment, and using books and print in our everyday lives is imprinting them with the importance of print. This is very different from those schools which think that all they have to do is to surround the children with good and attractive books and the children will learn to read them – presumably by some process akin to osmosis. If children are to be imprinted with the importance of print then it is essential that they see print in use.

It is important that parents look objectively at how they use print. In the days when everyone went to church regularly, when movies were silent but subtitled, when families sat around reading without radio or television, when newspapers were literate and largely unillustrated, when magazines and journals were essential for keeping in touch with a wider world, and when, in the absence of telephones, letters played a much more significant part in personal and family life, it was easy to demonstrate that reading was an integral and vital part of everyday life. Today, the moving wallpaper of TV is not so much a part of what was called 'the electronic global village', as a perpetual part of the plumbing. The mighty micros are not high-tech educators in the home, but often little better than amusement arcades in every living room. If the only reading done at home is by big brother or big sister relegated to their bedrooms to do their homework, to the accompaniment of trannie or walkman, then reading will have a negative status. Far better the home in which library books abound, magazines are read as a part of active interests or hobbies, and the TV and radio are only switched on after careful consultation of the published programmes.

When we mentioned to a distinguished paediatrician that we were writing this book she said, 'The most important thing to tell parents today is to cut the time children watch TV to half an hour a day.' The objection to TV is not the content of the programmes, which is sometimes excellent. What is wrong with TV for young children is that it is not interactive. Children will sit in front of it hypnotized by the moving colours, uncomprehendingly passive, in a state bordering on stupefaction. Of course, we understand that propping children in front of the TV set is safer than having them fall down stairs or bottom-shuffling in a busy kitchen, but it is far from ideal. The only interactive part of a TV set is the control panel and this is why young children discover it first and learn to play with it so quickly. The cure for all parents' problems with TV watching, therefore, is to switch the set off at the mains and leave it off, save for short, selected, suitable programmes.

To limit the use of TV to watching with father or mother also ensures that watching TV is interactive – it can be talked about, commented upon and asked about. Thus it can become another window on the world which, in turn, can be read about and written about, too. Many children get their first experience of reading when they learn to recognize the name of their favourite programme. But this is unlikely to happen with passive watching. If TV is to be seen by young pre-school children, the viewing should be limited to short sessions with their parents. Anything more than this is a waste of valuable learning time.

By the same token, of course, books should be used interactively by young children with their parents.

Reading – Silent, Aloud or for Action

Children regard being able to read as almost magical. Reading pictures they can understand. Pictures are usually something like the things they represent. Print is different. Someone thought of something first, then they expressed their thoughts in language and the language was written down. When we read what was written down we are reading what they thought. When people tell us things we have to understand what their words mean. So when we read, we must get to the meaning. But when we first start reading to children they do not fully understand this. Unlocking the meaning means unlocking the words. They are very literal and protest if we change one word in a well loved story we have read to them many times before. But the process is one which they also try to imitate by sitting down, as we sit down, and holding the book and turning the pages. If we have run our finger along the line of print they may try to do this too. They will look at the pictures and use them as cues to the narrative, possibly muttering to themselves, but usually intently 'reading' silently as this is what they have seen us do.

It is only by reading to children and by talking about what we have read that we begin to reveal the nature of this magical process. For what has to be revealed is that it is what goes on behind the eyes that is important. Then they will begin to understand that we do not 'look and say', as one method of learning to read was called. When we read aloud we 'look, think and say' and 'look and think' when we read silently.

Printed Language isn't Speech in Print

When father says to mother, 'Yes, we'll put it over there' mother knows what 'it' is and where 'there' is. The written instructions for the same purpose might be: 'The extractor unit should be mounted on the wall immediately above the cooker'. Printed language lacks concrete, situational cues to meaning. *Printed language, therefore, is more precise, formal and complex than everyday speech.*

Mother says to father, 'Saw your Gloria today. On the beach. Massive hat and minute bikini. No Fran. Odd. Carrying too much weight. And older. Just waved and yomped on!' Even Junior may get a clear message from that story, especially if he was on the beach and knows of Gloria and Fran. That language is very different from that used in the story books mother and father read to him: 'Once upon a time there was a beautiful princess. She had long golden curls and skin so fair she always wore a big green hat whenever the sun shone. . . .' *Printed language is clear, umambiguous and tries to tell you all you need to know so that you can imagine everything, even if you were never there.*

The biggest gap, however, is between the language used in print and the language used by young children. They find it very difficult to tell events in sequence, let alone to describe, or show the relationship between cause and effect. Children who can chatter away happily about what they are doing when they are doing it, become tongue-tied and monosyllabic if asked to tell us what they did and where they went only a few hours previously. They still need here and now, as well as their parents' Language Acquisition Support System (LASS), to help them.

It is for this reason that we cannot emphasize too strongly the importance of reading aloud to children so that they hear the more formal and carefully structured language of print. Not only does this help them to develop their own language, freed from the here and now of situation and gesture, but also to become familiar, before they start trying to read, with language in print.

In the process of listening to parents read to them, children also learn that print is arranged in lines which go down the page and which are followed from left to right across the page. Here print is lateral and lineal, whereas speech is temporal. Print is also different from pictures. Reading pictures is a skill they will also have learned as part of their lap-learning experience. Pictures are not just for looking at, they are for looking into. With pictures you can look there, and there, and examine the whole or the parts. Children learn to focus upon different parts of a picture as they explore it. Learning like this, to discriminate visually and to scan the lines of print from left to right, is helping to build up a picture of efficient reading and a model of all that is involved. If children have learned this in the first few years of life and have learned to love being read to, then they will have been brought to within an ace of cracking the code.

Reading at School

Reading at school can certainly continue these processes and many children who enter school at 5 years old quickly 'get the knack' if they haven't done so already. Teachers usually read to classes at least once a day and they usually try to hear children read, albeit briefly, each day. Children will also see other children at various stages of learning to read and this may well help them to see what it is that they need to do. Children's planned learning from other children is an activity under-used in most schools.

Where teachers find it difficult to compete with what the good parent can do is in the intimate and frequent interaction with the children. As we have seen, during the vital early stages of learning to read, progress is most rapid when children get concentrated periods of instruction.

Many children, too, find the noise and activity of school very distracting after the comparative quietness and orderliness of home. They may well find too much going on at once and too many exciting things distracting them. Teachers have to strike a difficult balance in maintaining an atmosphere which is controlled and relaxed, quiet and stimulating, free-and-easy and disciplined. At the same time, they have to balance individual attention and encouragement with group and class management and control.

It is only when children can read, write and spell that teachers can give them assignments of work or activities of an intellectual nature. This is certainly an incentive to teachers to get their classes reading. Unfortunately, even if everyone in a class can read, it is very unlikely that all children will be at the same level of reading. To meet this difficulty, reading primers, graded in order of difficulty, rather than real books, are used. These reading schemes certainly help teachers overcome the difficulties of supervising the reading of large numbers of children all at different levels of proficiency. It is highly debatable, however, whether they are as efficient as real books in advancing children's reading abilities. Often the children are kept in lock-step with the schemes, their only motivation being to read the next book because it is the next book. This is better than no motivation at all. But it demeans reading from an exciting and worthwhile activity to a mechanical and boring one. Little wonder that children who started school full of enthusiasm and interest complain that they don't like reading, or only want to read 'the next book' and have no interest in reading for enjoyment or for information.

Undoubtedly, therefore, children who start school able to read start with an enormous advantage which is greatly enhanced if they can read well enough to escape reading the pabulum of primers. Parents will have served their children well if their children have served their apprenticeship to reading and are already journeymen. Whether or not this process is completed before children start school, parents should continue to encourage and monitor their children's progress. We discuss this in detail in Chapter 9. This is particularly important if children are to develop the techniques of learning from reading and of studying.

Study Habits from Lap Learning

Study habits develop naturally out of lap learning. Whether our approach to lap learning is actually with our children curled up on our laps, sitting on our knees, propped up in bed or beside us in an easy chair with an arm around them, the essential characteristic of lap learning is that it is a warm, intimate, interactive learning environment in which the children are secure, happy and involved.

As they grow and mature – and get heavier – we should still try to keep the essential ingredients of lap learning, whilst providing our children with somewhere suitable for reading and writing. Although many children will curl up with books on the floor or somewhere particularly uncomfortable, if they are going to write it is essential that they are found a spot which allows them to adopt the correct posture and which enjoys good light. With this in mind, pick the best place from the outset. It helps if children get into the habit of sitting with us in one particular place when we read, play language games or when they write and spell. If it is not possible to combine all the right conditions in one place, then select one position for reading and reading activities and another for writing and other activities, such as puzzles or silent reading, which the child undertakes alone.

* Use the same place, at the same times, for the same activities, consistently and regularly.
* Choose somewhere quiet, light, away from distractions such as windows, TV.
* Choose somewhere where you can sit comfortably side by side, both able to see the book being read quite clearly.
* Choose somewhere with a level surface for writing on, at which the child may sit with correct writing posture (see pages 116–18).
* Wherever you choose, try to make being there as pleasant and enjoyable as possible, associated with success and a sense of purpose and achievement.

If the optimum conditions cannot be obtained without moving, building an extension, buying a desk, or massive reorganization of furniture, simply try to keep to one place where you both feel comfortable and at ease and can give your minds to having fun doing a job of work. Young children love being grown up and joining in adult activities such as washing-up, gardening – and reading. We must encourage them to feel that what they are doing is really important and is something about which they can feel proud. Taking pride in their achievement is something we must foster from the start so that it, too, becomes a habit. Each time they read with us, we want them to feel more confident and successful. Later, when they start to write, we will want them to try to make each letter better than the last. Children know that practice makes perfect, they experience this all the time, and it is our responsibility to harness this effectively to the task of learning to read, write and spell.

What we found in our own work with parents and children was that, once these work habits were established, they provided an excellent basis on which parents could help their children with assignments and homework from school or with their hobbies and other activities. The parents told us how their children seemed to enjoy working with them again. 'It was like the bond there was between us before he went to school,' one father explained. 'We'd helped him learn to swim and he was so pleased – not just with himself but with us. Since we've taught him to read, it's like that again. It's great when he calls out, "Will you give me a hand with this?" to whichever of us happens to be around.' Building good study habits is building a bridge, from learning for survival in infancy, to education for life in childhood.

Children as Communicators in Print

The children's drive to learn to read is only part of the bigger drive to be communicators. Born into a world of print, they not only want to crack the code to read the messages, they want to encode their own messages too. Parents help this drive when they encourage children to paint, model and draw and then to move on to tracing and copying letters and words. Clearly, the more parents can get the decoding and encoding going together in harmony, the better. Unfortunately, writing and spelling often lag a long way behind reading. There is no reason, however, why this should be the case and the attainment lag is not so much developmental as environmental: schools find it harder to provide the essential individual attention to writing and spelling skills than they do to reading. Although there are ways to overcome the difficulties experienced by teachers, parents can provide the best methods as well as the individual help and encouragement for their children. What has held many parents back from giving this help in the past has been their reluctance to interfere, especially as it has often been assumed that schools had special styles of printing and handwriting. In some instances, of course, this was the case. But many schools adopt a casual policy about handwriting and spelling, leaving it to the individual teachers to determine what methods, if any, are taught. Some teachers believe that what children have to say in writing is far more important than *how* they write it or spell it. This notion ignores the fact, conveniently for those who subscribe to it, that it is the responsibility of educators to equip children with the *means* of expression so that they can say whatever they wish to say in writing and be understood. It is a waste of money, in schools which have not enough cash for text books and library books, to provide micros for pupils who cannot spell or write legibly.

The failure of many schools to develop clear and efficient handwriting in the early years of schooling results in pupils of 11 and 12 years of age being incapable of taking down notes or of carrying out written work competently. Their poor spelling and unformed handwriting inhibit them from putting down what they know, and their consequent failure results in progressive alienation from school and education. Yet, in our experience throughout the education system, parents and employers, as well as colleges and universities, have spoken with one voice in urging schools to give greater attention to efficient and legible handwriting and accurate spelling. Not every child is capable of writing quickly in an elegant italic hand. Not every child will always spell *referred, preference, proceed, precede, accommodated* and *benefiting* correctly. But, properly instructed, all children can write fluently and clearly and can spell acceptably. Parents can teach their children to write and spell more effectively than those schools which have no policy and fondly imagine that spelling is 'caught not taught'. In the process, they will be helping their children to become better readers and more competent communicators with a lot more to say that's worth saying.

Good Parents – Active Apprentices

Being a good parent doesn't mean indulging our children by giving in to all their whims and demands. In fact, most parental explanations of their offspring's deviant or delinquent behaviours begin, 'We can't understand it – we've always given them everything they wanted!' It's a perfect recipe for disaster. Being a good parent is meeting a child's needs to the best of our ability in a warm atmosphere of mutual concern and respect for each other's interests and integrity, and setting clear and sensible limits for what is expected and what is acceptable. Children brought up in this way will, when they enter adolescence, be self-confident, cooperative, positive and secure, unlikely to be overanxious, and keen to work and to succeed.

Children whose parents neglect or reject them, or fail to set firm, clear limits for what is expected and is acceptable, are likely to enter adolescence as insecure, overanxious, bored and in a state of work-paralysis. Many parents, perhaps most of us, fall between the extremes of perfection and disaster, or we are only good in part! Before setting out on any new venture, such as teaching our children to read, it is just as well to check that we are going to make things better, rather than worse. There's a lot to be said, for instance, if you are a single-parent father of three children, with a job to hold down, for questioning the wisdom of embarking on a teaching programme with the youngest, a 3-year-old child. It's possible, however, that the eldest, aged 12, might make a very good job of it and stop pining so much for his mother. Alternatively, is there not someone else who would like the chance to help?

What we all should do is to ask ourselves if we are fully meeting our children's basic needs. A quick check through the list on pages 25 and 36 will indicate if we have got the balance about right. We also need to make sure that we can spare the time. Fifteen minutes to half an hour a day is very little providing, of course, we can embark on it full of energy and are able to enjoy it without feeling guilty that something or someone else is being neglected.

As parents, we don't teach in set periods, but incidentally and when we are needed, so that most of what we may do, may be done in short bursts of only two or three minutes. A little and often will certainly be most likely to suit 2- and 3-year-olds. But, however the time is divided up, it still has to be found and found daily. For most people it will be easier to set aside a regular time each day and work to some sort of routine, but others may prefer to fit in the reading and activities when opportunities present themselves. When we think of the pleasure and the help we are giving our children, it takes little resolve to make a decision and stick to it. Once started, our children's success will carry us through all the inevitable lets and hindrances.

Another decision which needs to be made is who is going to have the pleasure and privilege of doing the teaching. Father, mother, grandparent, elder brother or sister or A N Other? Or, would it be better to divide the responsibilities, one being in charge of the reading and directly associated activities, and the other in charge of the write and spell activities? We will discuss planning the programme later but it is as well to bear in mind now the sort of decisions which will need to be made. It is important that everyone involved is clear about the aims and objectives, the methods and materials. Once that has been achieved, then it is definitely a case of the more the merrier. It will become increasingly clear as the book goes on that two or three heads are better than a bit of one when it comes to reading.

With time and place, people and purpose agreed, and a check that we are meeting our children's basic needs, we must set our sights on adopting a style of teaching our children which will increase their self-esteem. As good parents it is the style which comes most naturally!

TEACHING STYLE FOR HIGH SELF-ESTEEM

* Be affectionate.
* Give security.
* Be consistent, reasonable and fair.
* Give opportunities for learning and finding out.
* Praise success.

In these ways, we will help our apprentices to become good journey-men.

4

What Reading Really Is

Reading is for Real

On a visit to Disneyland in Los Angeles, 2½-year-old Christopher
created a sensation. Down the main concourse ran the Three Little
Pigs. Christopher recognized them straight away and stood, trans-
fixed with delight, as they scampered past, squealing and squeaking
excitedly. Then, came the Wolf. As soon as he saw him, Christopher
let out a howl of rage, broke from his father's hand, and raced after
the Wolf. To the crowd's amazement and the Wolf's discomfort,
Christopher threw himself round the Wolf's leg yelling, 'No, Mister
Wolf, leave the Little Pigs alone!' The Wolf tried to shake Christopher off, but he clung on, shouting, 'No, leave the Pigs alone,
naughty Mister Wolf!' The crowd cheered. The Wolf growled. An
embarrassed father peeled a flailing Christopher from the Wolf's leg.
'Leave them alone!' Christopher shouted angrily as the Wolf steal-
thily, and greatly relieved, darted away to the boos of the crowd.

Although the pictures of the Pigs and the Wolf in the book
Christopher's parents had read to him were not particularly like the
larger-than-life Disneyland versions, Christopher was in no doubt
about who they were and what the Wolf was up to. For Christopher,
as for most young children, the stories we tell are real. Often the
stories are more real than reality. No wonder, therefore, that children love to be read to and want to read for themselves. By 3 years of
age, children who have enjoyed lap learning, such as Christopher
had enjoyed, have learned a lot about print, not least that reading is
for real when it comes to feelings, emotions, excitement, derring-do
and fantasy. They have learned a number of other things, too.

LESSONS LEARNED ABOUT PRINT IN LAP LEARNING

* Reading is enjoyable, useful and a way of communicating.
* You can represent things, which you have in your head, in colours and shapes on paper and other people will see and recognize what you drew or painted.
* Pictures in books mean, more or less, the same things to everyone. You can talk about them.
* Reading has meaning, just like speech.
* Printed language explains stories and describes things so clearly that you can imagine them in your mind just as if you were there when they happened, or as the writer saw or imagined them.
* Books open from right to left.
* Pictures and print usually go from top left to bottom right on each page.
* You look into pictures but you look along lines of print. Print goes from left to right.
* You can read aloud or read to yourself.
* You can act upon what you read.
* Print in books is like print in the street or around the house. There are things called words and letters.
* With great difficulty you can copy letters or words and even write your own name – if you are very clever.

Parents are continually being surprised at how seriously children of this age take their reading and at how much they know. It is also true, of course, that there is an enormous amount that they don't know. What frequently appears baffling is how children learn so much so quickly. We want to help them to learn more and it is around this stage, when they seem to learn so easily and are so eager to learn, that we want to help them to learn to read. We will be better able to help them if we understand the process of translating language into print.

Reading – an Overview

In this chapter we will examine each of the following key concepts:

1. Signs, pictures and symbols can be read and they make an excellent introduction to reading print and to writing.

2. The most important part of reading is guessing and not worrying too much about all the letters or their sounds.
3. Efficient readers skim along the tops of the lines and glance down the centre of the page.
4. If you don't know the language you can't read the print; if you know the language, reading print is easy.
5. The brain uses the eyes to scan, skim and skip print, seeking patterns of print and patterns of language.
6. If we know what it means before we read what it says, we'll know what it means when we've read it.
7. In learning to read, attention should focus on the context more than on the spelling.
8. We learn to spell when we learn to write.
9. Learning to read and learning to write should go hand in hand.
10. Reading, writing and spelling are skills which have to be performed automatically or they get in the way of communication.

If some of this is not quite clear, we have made one of our points already: 'if we know what it means before we read what it says, we'll know what it means when we've read it'.

Pictures, Signs and Symbols

Man began by making his mark as an *aide mémoire* to the route he had blazed through the jungle or to the number of animals he had. Here he was communicating with himself. When he wanted to communicate with others then he needed an agreed system. The earliest one to survive is the pictographic writing of Ancient Egypt. We use pictograms in our road signs for crossroads, Z-bends, or two-way traffic. Pictograms are fine for concrete things but abstract ideas present problems. The Chinese ideograms overcome this problem, but Chinese pupils have to learn between 3000 and 4000 signs. The big advantage of pictograms and ideograms is that you do not need to know how to speak the language in order to understand them. In the same way we can understand the Arabic numbers, for example, 7, 18, 305, whether we are English, French or Russian.

Like the Arabic number system which revolutionized mathematics, the business of writing down language was revolutionized by the invention of the first alphabet. Alphabets record, roughly, the sound of words in a simple code. But pictograms, signs and symbols still have the advantage of being readily understood and children enjoy using them. Whether it is a little drawing of a cat on a log for 'catalogue' or a heart to represent 'love', pictograms retain their usefulness and charm because they are universally recognizable and yet have the mystery of codes to be cracked. Commerce makes good use of them in marking fragile goods, labelling clothes with cleaning and washing instructions, whilst around the home and in our cars signs and symbols abound. It has even been suggested that British children should be trained and examined in their knowledge of signs and symbols, or what the proposers called 'graphicacy' – a move which would undoubtedly ensure that the pupils were thoroughly confused. Before the examiners get their paws on it, we can make sure that our children notice and understand as many signs and symbols in the world around them as possible. Not only will this introduce them to reading as getting meaning from print, it will also introduce them to the use of pictograms and ideograms in the arts, science and technology. We were once able to help a dyslexic youth to read simply by demonstrating to him how much he could 'read' already in mathematics and music, in both of which he was interested and able.

When children make drawings and paintings and tell us about them, they are already involved in the beginnings and the essence of the reading process. When they try to understand picture puzzles or rebuses in comics and puzzle books, they are actively decoding from one signal system of cues or clues to meaning. So the more games we play with them, which involve finding the meaning of puzzles or codes, the more we are familiarizing them with aspects of reading. As will be seen, we recommend the inclusion of such games in the reading activities and a number of games are given in Chapter 6 and in Appendix 6.

The Certainty of Guessing

Many parents have been shocked when we have suggested to them that guessing is an important part of reading. 'I don't want my son making wild guesses – I want him to know for sure!' protested one father. We pointed out that, first, we hadn't said anything about 'wild' guesses and that, secondly, if we showed him the word 'read', he'd have to guess whether it sounded like 'red' or 'reed'. In fact, when the Semites, on the Sinai peninsula, invented the first phonetic script around 1500 BC, it was a BCD rather than an ABC for it had no vowels. They took twenty-two signs from Egyptian pictograms to represent consonantal sounds. It isn't difficult to read English without vowels, especially as we have to guess what most of them sound like in any case:

.t .s n.t v.ry d.ff.c.lt t. .nd.rst.nd th.s, .s .t?

But, as every shorthand writer knows, leaving out vowels and the dots for them is something we can quickly get used to:

Ths cld b sd t b frctnlly hrdr t ndrstnd, bt, wth a lttl prctc y mght sn fnd tht y wr rdng t fstr thn f th vwls hd bn lft n!

It is not just a question of guessing the missing vowels, it is also a question of guessing what comes next in the message. Reading has been described as 'a psycholinguistic guessing game'. The print, those 'damn squiggly black marks', doesn't contain the meaning: it is a rough code for the sounds of the words behind which lies the meaning. Often we have to go on reading for quite a while before we reduce our uncertainty and are sure what the message means. You cannot know what this sentence means:

The bat in the bag with the gloves and pads was . . .

until it is completed. Only when you know how it ends can you decide its meaning. The bat was neither baseball nor cricket, but mammal and the last words, 'fast asleep', make that clear. From the very beginning, we want our children to guess the meaning of what they are reading with us because the most important lesson they have to learn is the one they know already: reading means finding meaning. It isn't, then, a question of wild guessing, but of making sense – that's the certainty of guessing.

Skimming over the Surface

The Greeks put vowels in the BCD and made the first ABC. Their modified alphabet, Cyrillic, went east to Russia. An Etruscan version of the Greek alphabet was taken up by the Romans and was spread by them and Europeans through the western world and beyond. The advantage of having vowels and well differentiated letter shapes is that they give more information than the bare essentials that we need. We can pick up the bits we want and, if we are ever in doubt and want to be absolutely certain, then we can use all the information. But this line of print makes it clear that it is the tops of letters which carry most of the information. When we efficient readers are reading, we are skimming over the surface, and over the tops of the lines in particular, just to pick up the cues we need to meaning. The revolution which the alphabet made possible – the efficient encoding of sounds into print – and the gradual evolution of the letter shape and spelling systems based upon it, has been so successful because print is a highly redundant system in which there's much more information 'on line' than we need. Most of the time we're just skimming the surface.

We will often mention the value of reading in a natural voice to our children while we run our fingers along the line of print. We want our children to have a model of efficient reading from the beginning. Efficient reading is skimming over the surface structure of print to find the deep meaning of language. How we do it so quickly depends on factors other than the ascenders and descenders of the letter shapes alone, but it clearly matters that, if our children are to become efficient readers, then the more accurately they can distinguish between letters and letter shapes, the faster they will learn to read. But this should not divert us from realizing that if you don't know the language you can't read the print.

No Language, No Reading

The very people to whom we owe our alphabet, the Etruscans, spoke a language which is dead and forgotten. Although Etruscan survives in written form, no one can read it. Etruscan is a lost language. Reading is not just making the right sounds for the right letters, although it is certainly part of the process. But barking at print isn't reading. We can bark at this, for example, but we cannot read it because it is not language but nonsense:

Blon moce enporfary, nevetiously wogtushed.

Attempting to teach children to read before they can understand and express themselves in language is both a waste of time and a way of putting them off wanting to read. Reading to children, on the other hand, is a way of teaching them language and of introducing them to reading. What parents do so successfully, as we have seen, is to teach language. That is how they make learning to read easy.

This is not to suggest that, if guided by a book such as Glenn Doman's *Teach Your Baby to Read*, parents who teach their children to respond to flashcards are likely to do their children any harm. But we would question how much children can read with limited vocabularies and would suggest that parents might be better employed playing the language game with their children. On the other hand, Dorothy Butler's *Cushla and her Books* has shown us what can be done to help a seriously handicapped child, her granddaughter, to acquire language through books. Many parents have demonstrated that teaching their handicapped children to read has transformed the children's language and other abilities. What we are stressing here is that if parents of all children, whether or not they have handicaps, recognize the importance of language and its meaning, then the letters and their sounds will fall into proper perspective. One aspect of that perspective is their direction.

The Brain Seeks Patterns

Early writers had to decide which way to put their symbols on the tablets or paper. For centuries, Chinese went from bottom to top of the paper. Now, like Japanese, Persian-based languages such as Arabic, as well as Urdu and Hebrew, it goes from right to left. The Greeks at one time wrote as they ploughed, going along one line from left to right and then back down the other line from right to left.
.ot desu teg ot tluciffid taht lla ton si ti ees nac uoy sA

Our reason for mentioning these facts is that there is no mechanism in the brain which demands that we should read one way and not another, whether we are right- or left-handed or ambidextrous. Reading is an acquired skill and, like all skills, requires practice. Certainly, like many other skills, such as talking or counting, it is more easily acquired when we are young, is best acquired in a way which is enjoyable and receives parental encouragement and support and, the sooner acquired, the sooner perfected.

But too much can be made about the importance of scanning print from left to right. Although the general direction is from left to right, our eyes do not move in a smooth flow but in a number of little grasshopper leaps, sometimes going backwards, only picking out those features of the text we need to get the meaning. Our eyes are not doing the reading but are obeying our brain which tells them what to look for. Fast readers scan down the centre of the page very much as we all scan down names in a directory. And we all have to scan quickly as the brain cannot get meaning if the letters or words come too slowly. We can get some idea of the difficulties experienced by children who have been taught by the 'finger prodding' method, and have to build up each word by sounding every letter or letter group, from these two lines:

I   t   i   s   n   o   t   a   t   a   l

l   e   a   s   y   t   o   r   e   a   d.

The brain reads patterns of print by the quickest and most economic means it can devise and it uses a variety of strategies to get to the meaning quickly. Without the pattern of letter and word shapes and the spaces between words, not to mention the different lengths of words, reading slows down so much it may soon become incomprehensible. Neither of these sentences is in code, but they have lost their familiar pattern of words:

WH ER EW ER ET HE YW HE NW EW ER EH ER E?

and

PLANO FFACT ORYEN CLOSE DINDI CATES STRAT EGICA LLYLO CATED SENSI TIVEI TEMSW EREQU IREPH OTOGR APHIN GSTOP

It is for this reason that reading ordinary books is far better than reading primers which use all the short little words that occur most frequently altogether. Not only is the language sure to be stilted, with neither the patterns of sense nor sound, but it is also bound to look odd and be harder to read quickly.

> Dan and Nan sat in a cab. Dan had a tan cap and Nan had a tan cat in her lap. The cab of the van that they sat in had a bed for Pat's pet rat and a cot for Nan's cat.

Some primers make a lot less sense than that. Primers are ideally suited for training children to read nonsense and, because they convince children that all they have to do is bark at the print they prod, without thought for its meaning, schools then have to teach 'comprehension' to convince them that they must also attend to the sense! Not surprisingly, it is at that stage that many children have decided school is a boring waste of time.

If we want our children to master the cues print gives to meaning we must help them to see the natural patterns of print. We can help this process by teaching them to write and spell so that they learn the patterns of strings of letters with the patterns of words as they learn to write their own thoughts. When they are reading we want them to concentrate upon the patterns of language. This is using their brains to train their eyes. Reading is more a matter of what goes on behind the eyes than of what is in front of them.

Reading Means Meaning

We have seen how the visual patterns of print help us to process it quickly. Knowing what the message means and understanding how the words used in language follow one another in a pattern is even more important. A sentence begins, 'Once upon a time . . .' or 'Thank you for . . .' or 'Although there . . .' or 'If I were . . .' and we can all anticipate the sort of sentences which will follow. We anticipate patterns of grammar and even some of the words which may follow.

But to play the psycholinguistic guessing game and win, we need to know what the message means before we read it. Certainly, as parents, we want to be sure that our children will understand and enjoy what they read. But many parents find it hard to grasp the concept that we need to know what the message means before we read it. We can put ourselves in the child's position by trying to read these sentences, one or two of which some of us may find difficult:

> Conversion requires the act amount to denial of the plaintiff's title but detinue does not. Replevin is a third tort against chattels.

> Finding derivatives of functions assists in finding primitives.

> Convalency exists in the hydrated proton when a spare pair of electrons in the H_2O molecule forms a bond with a positively charged hydrogen ion or proton.

> Immurement in the dorter induced aboulia and velleity so that the antonomasia for the grallatorial noumenon eluded her.

Of course, we may get help from a dictionary but, without knowledge of the subjects – the law, mathematics, physics or whatever – we will still need help to reach full understanding. Not that the syntax or the vocabulary need to be difficult. Scholars still argue about the meaning of Hamlet's 'To be or not to be', many parents would be stumped in distinguishing between Miss Muffet's curds and whey, and we may need to read these simple words by Gertrude Stein more than once to unlock their meaning:

> Any one not coming to be a dead one before coming to be an old one comes to be an old one and comes then to be a dead one as any old one comes to be a dead one.

By reading to and talking with our children we help to overcome these difficulties of gaining meaning. Their questions and our explanations help to bridge the gap. Thus we also demonstrate how context can be used to find meaning, how one word or phrase may give a cue to the possible meaning of another. At the same time we are also showing that reading can enlarge our understanding. This is the beginning of learning from reading. But, in the early stages of reading, we strongly recommend that children should never be asked to read anything that they do not already understand. Later, they should never be asked to read aloud something they have not first had an opportunity to prepare. Our method of following paired reading with prepared reading ensures that our children will know what they read when they read it. Later, we will refer back to this concept when we discuss the importance of the Language Experience approach.

Context Counts More than Spelling

So far we have spoken about our alphabet as phonetic, as if our letters stood for sounds and that was all there was to it. Unlike German, Welsh, Scandinavian and Slavonic languages, the English language is not blessed with an alphabet which is phonetically consistent. Sometimes some of our letters don't make a sound: The Lam*b H*otel, for example. In some words the same letter may make two quite different sounds, as in *circle* or *garage*. For decades British schools used a word recognition test to obtain children's Reading Ages – another example of nonscience invented by educationists – which contains the only word in the language in which the letters *olo* make the sound *er*. Unfortunately, many of the children who said the word correctly, and thereby added a month to their Reading Ages, thought the word had something to do with nuts. The word, of course, is colonel.

Although children may have difficulties with spelling when they are writing, when they are reading we do not want them to be looking at and worrying about the individual letters and their sounds. We are sure many parents read 'circle' and 'garage' without consciously distinguishing between the sounds of the 'c's or 'g's. The following sentence demonstrates how unimportant spelling is when we read:

> On the quay we could see one of these people seize the key to the green machine and give it to the chief officer who threw it in the sea.

The fact that the sentence contains examples of all the different ways of spelling the long 'ee' sound matters not at all. Had we heard it read aloud, we would not have been helped by the different spellings of 'key' and 'quay' or of 'sea' and 'see'. The context, not the spelling, gives the meaning when we listen to speech. When we read print, with its high redundancy of letters and particularized spelling, it is still the context which we rely on to give us the meaning.

Meaning Means Speed

By making the process of reading an automatized and speedy process from the beginning, we help our children to get the knack and get it all together from the start; in other words, we help them to begin as they will go on. By taking attention away from the spelling and sounding, we focus upon meaning and making sense. *By scanning and skipping and skimming, the children are not looking at the parts of a sentence but at the whole. Because the whole is greater than the sum of the parts, we call our approach* a **holistic approach** *to reading*. But we do not throw the baby of phonetics out with the bathwater of phonics and sounding. These subskills, as they are called, are also learned automatically in the writing and spelling patterns and in the games and activities.

When we reflect on it, our analogy of learning to ride a bike carries the same message: until our cyclist is moving forward fairly fast, he is in grave danger of falling off. Similarly, until the skills of spelling and writing are automatized, the child is like the cyclist whose lack of speed causes him to wobble. But it is only when our cyclist is competent that he can look around him and appreciate the scenery or concentrate upon where he is going. Automatized skills of reading, writing and spelling enable our children to think about the meaning and enjoyment of what they are reading or writing and to concentrate upon what they want to find out or communicate.

Reading – the Holistic Model

It is obvious that the child who embarks upon learning to ride a bike or to read has to be strongly motivated to do so. What is often forgotten is that the child has to be motivated by the activity itself to carry on with it. Reading has to be self-rewarding. If we don't enjoy what we are reading or if we don't find the information we are looking for, then we soon stop reading. Particularly important in the beginning stages of reading, although it holds true throughout our lives, is that we should understand what we read. It is from that point that we begin our definition of reading.

> Reading is the self-rewarding, cultural activity of participating in the retrieval of thought and language encoded in alphabetic symbols by the automatized scanning of print for the purpose of finding its meaning.

This model describes the process and its purpose, the gaining of meaning. From it we can derive our model of writing:

> Writing is the cultural activity of participating in the recording of thought and language in alphabetic symbols for the purpose of communicating meaning.

Both activities are participatory because, unless we think about what we are reading or writing, we will fail to realize their purposes. They are participatory cultural activities because everything we read or write, no matter how trivial or profound, in some way derives from our cultural heritage and linguistic environment. The definitions may appear daunting but, we suggest, anything less would fail to do justice to the importance and value of the skills, or would mislead us into starting with a simplistic view of them, which would diminish the abilities and the dignity of our children. Fortunately, it is the very rigour of this analysis of the process of reading, and the way in which it goes hand in hand with the skills of writing and spelling, which enables us to devise ways and means of making learning to read by reading easy, sensible and successful.

Talking into Reading

The teaching of reading is a natural extension and development of the language game parents play so successfully that all children grow up speaking their 'mother tongue'. We talk to them and with them, and they learn to understand and to express themselves in language.

We read to them and with them, and they learn to read. In the process of reading with them we explain and discuss what we have read, thereby helping to make the printed form of language accessible and significant to them. Clearly, Christopher had participated in the cultural activity of reading with his parents the story of The Three Little Pigs. How could a 2-year-old understand the Wolf's intentions, let alone recognize a larger-than-life wolf, save through the conversations of his parents?

It is essential that throughout the process of learning to read, parents continue to talk with their children about reading and studying. This will ensure that reading is fully integrated into our children's thought, language and intellectual development. We will discuss later the ways in which this may be done with older children; here we wish to stress the importance of an on-going dialogue between us and our children as they learn to read, so that we can help them learn the techniques of reading and be active participators in the development of their own language and understanding.

Another reason why conversation is so important is that we just do not know how children learn to read or why some fail to learn. Learning to read involves getting together such a complex of sub-skills, skills and higher-order skills to work in harmony with memory, imagination, motivation and intellect that the wonder is that anyone learns it, rather than that a few don't. What we know is that some children can be helped to learn by one way, some by another. With the interplay of many factors, too, some children experience difficulties in aspects which other children take in their stride. Some children have difficulties which have nothing to do with the reading process, but with their learning abilities or with their styles of learning. Children who are impetuous and impatient may attack reading so impulsively that they enjoy initial success which they might have difficulty in sustaining. Cautious and overanxious children may simply fail to learn not because they lack ability, but because they do not wish to make mistakes. If we are to allow for all the different ways in which our children learn then we should say 'vive la différence' at the outset and make sure that, having a big enough model to accommodate all their difficulties and differences, we can talk them through to success. Reading is only language; we must use it to help our children learn the skill.

MODES of Reading

We had to face this problem of the different ways in which individual children learn to read some years ago when we were invited to design the first Computer Assisted Teaching Project for the teaching of reading to children in the 7-plus age range. The system we designed allowed each child to learn according to his or her preferred way and at his or her own rate. Children progressed along the Main Mode or route, or along other Modes or routes which converged upon the Main Mode, when they were able to use it to advantage. The five Modes were:

M Main Mode: learning to read by reading for meaning.
O Orthographic and Calligraphic Mode: learning to read by learning to write and to spell.
D Dialogue Mode: learning to read through talking with a teacher who stimulated, motivated and gave a feeling of success.
E Language Experience Mode: learning to read by writing stories and expressing oneself in print.
S Subskills Mode: learning to read by decoding meaning from print and encoding language in writing.

In each of the Modes of the CAT Project were the books, aids and resources, arranged in order of difficulty, to be used by the pupils. The purpose of the computer program was to save teachers' time by identifying, according to each pupil's progress, the next books or tasks they might need. The aim of the Project was to free teachers so that they could devote their time and energies to interacting with the children and to giving them individual help and support as and when they needed it.

More recently, when we developed the programmes to be used by parents with their children who had been identified, by independent specialists, either as dyslexic or, by their headteachers, as severely retarded in reading, we built on our experience with the Modes of the CAT Project. We designed games and activities which could be used by the parents, in association with paired reading with the children, to overcome and prevent difficulties, and to accelerate their progress in learning to read. In this one-year DES-funded action research project, all thirty children in our experimental groups made progress: eleven pupils made two to three years' progress; ten pupils made three to four years' progress; and one pupil made four years' progress. In contrast to these significant gains in reading made by the majority of the dyslexic and reading-retarded pupils, only two of the fifteen pupils in the control group matched with them had made one year's progress in the year; the remainder were further behind in their reading than they had been at the beginning of the year. The success of the pupils in the experimental groups is directly attributable to their parents. Pupils in the control group had received no planned parental help.

In the light of this success, we analysed the results and found, to our surprise, that each of the activities and games was considered by some children and their parents to have played a particularly significant part in helping them learn to read. This may not be surprising so far as writing and spelling activities or word games are concerned. It certainly is surprising that some children found learning nonsense verses and comic verses helped them most of all. And, although dyslexic pupils are thought to have particular difficulty with encoding and decoding language, it is surprising that some of them enjoyed and considered they were helped most of all by writing and deciphering messages in 'secret' codes. This evidence confirmed us in our belief that the things children enjoy doing with their parents can all contribute, either directly or indirectly, to success in reading.

The parents in this action research project may well have been a select and special group. Certainly, many of them were strongly motivated. Their children, all between the ages of 9 and 13, had known years of failure. But it was idle to speculate when we could readily try the same approaches, based on the same holistic model of reading, and find out how other parents and their children responded to them. This we have done with parents from a wide range of social backgrounds and circumstances with a wide range of children of different ages and abilities. The results have not only confirmed the effectiveness of the methods, but have confirmed the experience of other experimenters working, like ourselves, directly with parents and their children.

In the next chapter, therefore, rather than tell people what they ought to do, we prefer to describe in detail what parents have done that has worked. With the knowledge of the process of reading we have already described, readers will be able to see for themselves how and why the various methods, approaches, activities and games have played their part. Having learned what other parents have done, readers will then be able to start adapting and adopting the recipes for reading which best help them and their children to provide a healthy diet.

5

How Parents Teach Reading – Lap Learning

Good parents teach reading by interacting with their children in exactly the same way as they teach them so successfully to walk and to talk. They respond to their children's changing demands and interests, they stimulate new interests and provide new opportunities. But they don't force the pace and they don't demand that their children perform precisely to a developmental timetable. Good parents are realists and know that if their children are happy and are eating and sleeping reasonably satisfactorily, there is no point in making them miserable by trying to force feed them in order to accelerate their growth or their development. A child's active enjoyment is the parents' best barometer. We stress this because, if parents attempt to change their teaching strategies in order to teach reading and try to make children conform to their wishes, they will do more harm than good. Fortunately, the younger children are, the more immediate and explicit their reactions, and they will push a book away if they don't like it or have had enough of it, as vigorously as they will push away a spoonful of stewed prunes they don't want.

The two approaches which parents have found most effective are 'learning to read by reading' and 'learning to read by writing'. But it should not be assumed that every child will follow either of these lines of development in the order given here, or that every child will develop along the lines of both approaches simultaneously. Rates of progress will vary from child to child and for each child; and some children will skip stages, others will seem to stick at one stage forever. For example, many children can read fluently but are not able to say their ABC, whilst others can say and write letters and simple words before they can read the simplest book. Each child and parent will find their own route together. The child will lead, the parent will prepare the way, encourage and point out the attractions which lie ahead. And the starting point is when the child starts pointing!

Starting Point – Pointing

Somewhere around 9 to 18 months children start to point at things. They may well make sounds as they do so, as if naming the things although they do not necessarily use words. They will stab at moving things and follow them with their eyes. At about this time, too, speech is emerging and children often have an accessible passive vocabulary of words they recognize correctly, although they may not be able to say them. We will know this because they respond appropriately to the words. They often look puzzled when really they are thinking. When they are puzzled, they are likely to laugh. Point to a chair and say 'Mama' and they will look puzzled, possibly thinking, 'Do they mean Mama's chair?' Point at an ear and say 'ear' and then at a hand and say 'chair' and they will laugh at the incongruity.

When parents know that children know that objects are constant and stand out from other objects, they start the naming game and it is around this time that they produce the children's first books. The books are usually rag books or board books, physically rugged, hygienic and with 'safe' colours, with simple pictures usually of everyday things or animals. As, at this age, most children put things straight in their mouths and chew on them, rag and board books need to be tough and safe. Children often need a period of familiarizing play with them, dropping them so that they disappear, or throwing them about. Then parents sit the children on their knees and turn over the pages, naming the objects depicted as they do so. This may well be an occasion for pointing or stabbing at the pictures. Some children may imitate their parents' words, others may know and attempt to say the names of the objects, some will not respond at all and others will push the book away. If the book arouses interest, the game continues until attention wanders; if not, it is put aside for another day. Until the children enjoy the pictures and show signs of wanting to turn the pages over, most parents do take the books away, rather than leave them to be treated as toys or teething rings.

At this stage the value of these books is largely as another opportunity for talking and looking together. In part, however, as the children's first books, they are their introduction to books, to pictures and to turning over from right to left, and most parents want to see these aspects established and enjoyed.

Go for clear, colourful realistic pictures, preferably without fussy backgrounds, of common everyday things and pets. Children have not yet learned to read pictures and, as their first experience, it is novel and interesting. Many parents cut out pictures from magazines, cutting round the shape of an apple or dog which is then pasted on to a piece of plain paper or card so that it stands out clearly. In the course of a few weeks it is possible to build up a boxful of pictures like this and, as the children's interest and ability to read pictures develops, so the pictures may gradually become more complex. By this we mean, simply, that two similar or different objects might be mounted on the same card. In the early stages overlapping objects, for example, may cause confusion.

One important aspect of reading pictures is the big jump between realistic pictures and outlined diagrammatic ones, a jump which children only gradually learn to make. In choosing pictures and books we need to ask ourselves how far the child has gone along this line of recognition:

DEVELOPMENT OF RECOGNITION OF OBJECTS

* Recognizes, say, real cup when presented for drinking.
* Recognizes cup used for drinking when on shelf.
* Recognizes cups as a general group of objects.
* Recognizes model cup – as in toy set.
* Recognizes realistic picture of cup on its own.
* Recognizes picture of cup amongst other clearly depicted objects.
* Recognizes object when only significant part – say half of cup with handle visible – is shown.
* Recognizes outline drawing of cup.

Many attempts have been made to produce attractive photographs of objects for children but most parents find that, no matter how much *they* may like them, children prefer simple, colourful, realistic pictures without obtrusive backgrounds.

As children become familiar with pictures and begin to name them, parents tend to take the game a step further. The child says, 'Cat', and the parent says, 'Yes, a black cat', and later, 'Yes, like our tabby . . .' and the child completes the sentence with 'cat' or its name. What seems to happen is that parents judge just how to push the game a little bit further to make it more interesting and valuable. They have helped the child to name things, now they are distinguishing between the characteristics of things – their colour, how big or small they are, where they are or what they are doing. Once this dialogue has been started with simple pictures and with rag and board books, the children will be seeing pictures in the world around them, in advertisements, on packets. Soon they will be ready for the next step, looking at picture books, but already they will have begun the apprenticeship to becoming hooked on books.

Picture Books – Visuals of Rhythm and Rhyme, Story and Song

This is a vital stage but, for light relief, a warning about believing experts! We wondered just when parents began playing Pat-a-Cake and games such as This Little Pig Went to Market in which they spoke or sang whilst performing actions with their children. The research and our own observations confirmed that many mothers start within hours of the birth and certainly when they begin washing and changing their babies, which led us to wondering whether they started before birth. It didn't take long to discover that, of course, serenading and finger-tapping on the Delectable Dome is a ritual in which both parents are known to participate. Dr Anthony DeCasper of the University of North Carolina has found, moreover, that unborn babies, happily floating in the amniotic fluid, appear to remember and, after birth, show a preference for their mothers' voices. Now we think there may be something in this research which warrants further investigation, but what we found harder to accept was this: Dr DeCasper got a group of pregnant women to read to their foetuses from Dr Seuss's *The Cat in the Hat*. Subsequently, he found that, after birth, the children preferred listening to *The Cat in the Hat* rather than to another book. This, we suggest, may only demonstrate that the children preferred *The Cat in the Hat* in the same way most children do – it's a wonderful book!

Language sounds carry meaning in words, but they also carry meaning in the sounds themselves. Volume, rate and rhythm all convey meaning. Shout at a newborn child and we get the startle reflex, coo and the child quietens. So what children learn from our early games with them is a great deal of knowledge of human communication of emotion and feeling. Gentle progress with a steady rhythm of our fingers on their bodies lulls them, but when suddenly the rhythm changes, they are surprised into gurgling with delight. Jiggle and joggle them gently on our knees as we sing 'This is the Way the Farmer Rides' and, no matter how many times they have experienced it before, they will hoot with laughter when the galloping starts. What Daniel Stern has called 'the pure interaction' of mother and baby becomes formalized into games and increasingly directed to developing verbal communication.

Rhythm, exaggerated in nursery rhymes and lullabies, is a physical and sensory experience which communicates precisely the emotions it is expressing – from soothing, soporific, gentle rocking through smooth, competent handling to angry, jerky, violent shaking. The greater the variety of rhythms children experience in their songs, rhymes and games, the more aware they become of them. They, in turn, will have a greater variety of behaviours, be better able to distinguish between the rhythms of speech, and more sensitive to rhythm in language and music. When rhythm and rhyme combine in the well worn pebbles of language, the nursery rhymes and songs, they are communicating our culture in one of its most memorable modes. Yet we have heard teachers exclaim to children of 6, 7 and 8 years old, 'Stop that babyish sing-song chanting' at the very time when they should have been using, nurturing and extending rhythm and rhyme. Meanwhile researchers have to rediscover the gold which once lay upon the surface and exclaim 'Eureka!' as they dig it up from beneath the detritus of miseducation.

The singing of songs with simple story lines, such as Jack and Jill, Three Blind Mice, Humpty-Dumpty, and the telling of simple tales such as The Three Little Pigs, often accompanied by actions and acting, with the rhythms sustaining them and the rhymes binding them together, provides a rich seed-bed in which language flourishes. Once these tales and rhymes have been learned and repeated many times, many parents give them a new lease of life by showing their children pictures illustrating scenes from them. Now words from the songs are used in conversation. 'Look, there's Humpty – where's he sitting? He sat on the . . .' says parent, and 'Wall', says child. Or the child makes a completely irrelevant noise and parent sings the line, 'Humpty-Dumpty sat on the wall' and the child may join in – or turn the page impatiently. It just doesn't matter. All that matters is the interaction. Often, parents later realize, the children who had sung with them so sweetly had never really understood at all. This doesn't matter either, for the books demonstrate that they are revelatory and make all plain at last.

Now children of 1 and 2 years of age are learning to look at and into pictures. It will still be important that they are not confused, artily impressionistic or grotesque pictures, but children will enjoy finding the fox or looking for birds in the trees or the characters in 'Who Killed Cock Robin?' if the scene is not too cluttered. Research has shown that even 7-year-olds have difficulties in gaining information from pictures, so our concern for clear, bold, colourful pictures for very young children is understandable. Talking with parents, two main problems emerge: it is important that the children actively enjoy the pictures; it is important that the parents like the books. The worst books are what we call 'auntie books' which are designed and produced to look fashionable and are overpriced *kitsch*, child equivalents of coffee-table books designed to impress the impressionable. Save your money, tell auntie 'book tokens next time', and go for the cheapest and clearest that you think your child will like. The universal success of the Dick Bruna books demonstrates that simplicity need not be crude or bland.

Some of the books in this category may well have small bits of text and this can safely be ignored for the time being. However, they do serve two useful purposes in reminding parents who have forgotten the rhymes or tales and in providing a future opportunity for reading together. What is needed at this stage is that the pictures should tell the story or illustrate the key characters of nursery rhymes which have already been enjoyed and sung together. Now, if the pictures are clear, colourful and graphic, we want them to come off the page and proclaim themselves. These pictures help to clothe the imagination of the child – how else could children test whatever it was they thought was meant by 'The mouse ran up the clock'? It doesn't matter, therefore, if different books show different interpretations or depictions of the rhymes. This will help the children to realize that the story or rhyme remains the same, but we may imagine it in a variety of ways. When Christopher attacked the larger-than-life Wolf, you will recall, he clearly had imagined it for himself but could identify, too, with a completely different depiction.

Parents' retelling of the rhymes and stories and their interaction with their children has established that books are to be enjoyed and are enjoyable. We have written as if parents are spending hours each day doing this, when, of course, they may never spend more than a few minutes each day. The parents who are most successful are the ones who enjoy it most themselves. Sometimes we suspected that the children were unlocking hidden dramatic or comic talents in their parents. What clearly matters most for the children is the intensity of the enjoyment whenever it is experienced. As we can see, there has been a progression from the simple pictures of the rag and board books which demonstrated the naming of things and their representation of them. Now the language of stories and rhymes they already know are being portrayed and can be used as prompts for more language, whether in conversation about the pictures or in a repetition of the originals. This stage moves almost imperceptibly to the next, in which the pictures, in sequence, tell old and new tales.

Picture Story Books

As children's language abilities develop and their world expands, thanks to their increasing mobility and dexterity, the need for stories grows. Between 18 and 36 months, children are learning so rapidly that they need language to order their thoughts, and stories to order reality. At its most simple a story is a happening. Young children are surrounded by happenings over which they have little or no control. Stories sort things, happenings, out. They have a beginning, a middle and an end. Picture books which show a sequence of events, often very trivial to the adult mind, fascinate children and feed a real need. The passage of time, the changes in the scenes of a journey, a cause and its effects, are central cores around which reality is given some semblance of order for children.

Simplicity and clarity of depiction is still important. The fantastic is acceptable because, at this age, almost everything is fabulous, but the grotesque and frightening should be avoided. Many children have told their parents, as they switched out the light at night, 'Turn the book over – don't let the witches/robbers/giant out!' Reading is real, and in such circumstances it is not difficult to reassure children. Where pictures have been deliberately contrived to frighten, some children can be literally terrified by them. This is very much an individual matter, and a sweet little girl may dismiss a picture which a tough little boy finds repellent. Parents are far better being guided by their children in matters of taste than by fashion, provided that they also take time to understand, and then extend and develop, their children's sensitivity to as wide a range of experience as possible. A matter-of-fact interest is best. As parents we want our children to be robust, not mawkish.

Picture story books, then, are for talking through, with the children taking an increasing part under the guidance of their parents. Language now will be much more particular and specific, and both parents and children will ask more searching questions requiring more elaborate answers. It is something that parents are uniquely good at because they are unselfconscious and their minds are usually uncluttered with jargon and generalizations. They are thinking with and for their children. Now, if father asks, 'Where's the fox?' the child of 2 years or over may well reply, 'He's hiding behind the hedge so's the hen won't see him', rather than point. But, if the child should only point, then the chances are that father will provide the answer and move on to something else. But the child will have heard the little function words – *the, so, behind, of, at, and, or* etc. – which we use to weave words together. Talking through picture books helps to draw attention to these important, busy little words. This is because pictures pin things down on the page. The frame of parent-child interaction and the frame of the picture hold events so that we can talk about them and examine them. This is often difficult to do in real-life situations because speech flows on in time. It is virtually impossible to do with TV's fast-moving images. Books like Eric Hill's *Spot* books invite just this sort of fun of looking and talking together in a way which focuses attention and makes language sharper and more particular and specific.

Research has shown that many children have difficulty in learning to read at 5 and 6 years of age because they had not previously realized that these little words existed, let alone what their functions were. They had relied so much on gesture and imitation that they were largely dependent upon the contexts of situations to get meaning. We remember one 6-year-old suddenly exclaiming in class, 'Skuze!' Only when he stood up and began writhing was it realized that his strange sound stood for, 'Please may I be excused?' Parents who talk their children through picture story books help their children to understand and use these words in the context of pictures, which their children enjoy, and in the context of books, which promise even greater enjoyment as the children develop.

Some of these picture story books will depict rhymes and tales they already know, others will introduce exciting new characters and stories. Going from the known to the unknown is a natural sequence and, although children at this age will soon get fixated on one particular book which they demand be read over and over again – and we should respect this need – the greater the variety, the better. It is only through variety of experience that we discover the uniqueness of our children, their talents and strengths, their interests and insights. Some girls and boys, for example, at this age want to look at how things move or are made, and find fascination in the factual. Already, browsing in the library or a good children's bookshop may help them to discover what interests them.

Many of these books will have print, just a few lines of the 'story' on each page. Some children will want the print read, others may display no interest in it. If the books are used primarily for their pictures and conversation, then reading the text can be counted a bonus. Some children may well cut their reading 'teeth' on these books and need little more, while other children, who are in no way less able, will need many years of exposure to print before they read. This should not worry or even concern parents at this stage if their children are actively enjoying looking at the pictures and talking about them, in so far as they are able to talk at all. As we have seen, looking at pictures requires a lot of skill. It is only yesterday, in terms of man's long history, that we invented perspective in pictures.

What will undoubtedly be noticed by some children at this stage is that there are words and letters, shapes and sounds. Parents don't need to teach these, of course, but using them, and helping the children to understand them, plays a big part in preparing children for reading. Children who are unfamiliar with words such as *word*, *letter*, *sound*, *sentence* have been found to be at a big disadvantage when it comes to learning to read. When playing games such as 'Where's the . . .?', 'Find the . . .', 'Hunt the . . .' and later I Spy, with picture story books will provide many opportunities for using these and other words which help us to talk about language.

Somewhere around this stage parents often introduce children to their first ABC and number books. We think they have a very real and important place, but precisely *when* will vary enormously from child to child. Many children learn to read, count and compute without them.

Alphabet Picture Books

When children are happily receptive to looking at big bold pictures and are already talking, it soon becomes clear that it is useful to know the names of the letters of our alphabet. When, at around 3, 4 and 5, children want to write their own names, this may well be soon enough to learn. If children are interested in them, they will play with educational toys incorporating letter shapes and soon start using the letter names. What all children need to know is that, just as there is a family of things called vegetables or fruit or furniture, so there's a family called the alphabet or ABC. Drawing and write-and-spell patterns will play a big part in making sure that they know the letters and their sounds. The best function ABC books can perform is that of making a happy discovery and a pleasant introduction to letters big and small. The books should be treated as picture books and will have served their purpose if they help to establish, in a pleasant way, that letters are there ready and waiting to be used when they are needed. Their first use may well be in the very important task of writing the children's names, or in recognizing a word the children see in advertisements, or in playing Grandmother's Cat.

What we say here about ABC books applies to number books. The children will first meet counting, no doubt, as they take their first steps or, even earlier, when parents walk their fingers over them. Going up steps or stairs is another favourite counting time. So a 'first number book' serves as an introduction to what the numbers look like. It may be some time, however, before children will have grasped the underlying mathematical concepts. This is of no importance if we use numbers to count on and count back, and in all the thousands of everyday situations from telling the time and date to measuring. It is the concrete experience of using one, two, three or first, second, third, and so on, and of learning the names of shapes, which will stand them in good stead. Parents, without attempting to hurry their children forward, should not make the mistake of thinking that number concepts develop inside children to be laid like eggs according to some Piagetian cycle. Experience and language, in this case the language of mathematics, must develop together. Most of us have to use concepts we will never fully understand, but what we do know is that parents who play number games, whether with dice, dominoes, cards, shells or abacus are doing a wonderful job.

Alphabet books need to meet a number of essential tests:

* Clear pictures of known, recognizable things, for example, apple.
* Capital and small letters. A, a.
* Type faces which clearly differentiate between letters. I, i, l.
* Short simple bold text. An apple. An A for an apple.
* Well laid out, uncluttered page.
* Direct humour or unpretentious simplicity. An A for an apple a day.
* Funny or fascinating.

Some alphabet books give each letter in a variety of its different styles, including the cursive or handwritten form. Others, like the delightful *ABC of Things* by Helen Oxenbury, create zany humour by combining things in juxtaposition like her juggler juggling jelly and jam. If we bear in mind the language known by the children and their ability to read and enjoy pictures, we shall have no difficulty in making a match.

Alphabet books are best used like all the other books we have described so far: for looking at and talking through together. Once that has been done they may become the basis for games such as 'Find the letter Q . . .', or 'Where's the umbrella . . .?', or 'How many things beginning with . . .?' Now the children are using the book very much as a reference book, turning the pages and searching them. Whether or not parents will want their children to learn the alphabet now or later depends partly on how able the children are with their writing, and partly on how keen they are to learn it. Chanting the alphabet without knowing which letter is which won't do any harm but, with so much that children want to learn and can usefully learn, this is rather pointless. The prime purpose of the alphabet book is to introduce the letters, their sounds and the alphabetic system in a pleasant manner. Before learning them, the children may need to have a lot more experience of language, its meaning and its sounds, and concrete experience of handling and making 3D and 2D shapes.

Parents who find their children are fascinated by letters, their sounds and shapes, can cut out letters in all their shapes and sizes and stick them, together with cut-out pictures, to make their own alphabet cards. Later, when the children are learning to write, these may prove very helpful. One point to watch is that we always make it quite clear which way up the cards should be held if there is no picture to make this obvious. One child got very confused by a picture of a playful puppy rolling on its back to illustrate the letter p – she'd always held it up the other way and said 'd for dog'! A line under letters, such as b, d, m, n, o, p, q, s, u and x, can be used to make clear which way up they should be if the picture or capital letter doesn't do so. A ball is a ball whichever way we look at it. As we shall see later, children have to learn to perceive how things are orientated in space, and this ability is slow to develop.

By introducing children to the ABC, they become much more aware of print around them on advertisements, labels, signs, etc. They can now ask, 'What does that say?' or 'Is that a W?' Some years ago, some teachers discouraged parents from teaching children the names of the letters. They thought the children should first be taught their sounds. In our experience, and today most teachers would agree, parents are perfectly able to teach both! By the time the first ABC books have been introduced, parents will have ample opportunity to introduce the names and sounds of letters in trying to satisfy their children's curiosity about print around them or in trying to arouse their interest in games such as I Spy. In both situations it will soon arise that some letters have more than one sound and that some are sometimes silent. Parents usually teach the useful things first – it's in their own interests!

The First Story Books with Pictures

'And what is the use of a book,' thought Alice, 'without pictures or conversations?' Alice's author knew what he was writing about, but he also knew that, whilst the pictures and conversation may entice the children, it is the story which holds them in its web. These first story books may well have big pictures and a small amount of text, but the acid test of them is that they should tell rattling good tales. This way lies *War and Peace*, Homer's *Odyssey*, *Tom Sawyer*, *Catch 22*, *Treasure Island* and *Tom Jones*. Until now books have been looked at and talked through. These books are for reading through. Now the parents' aim is for rapt absorption on the part of the child who is hanging on every word. Just how important this 'hanging on every word' is has been brought home to us many times. Sometimes, when reading to children, we've substituted a simpler word. Later, reading the story again, possibly for the fourth or fifth time, we've inadvertently read the correct word – only to be corrected by the child who insists on the word we used before.

Of course, the story, its characters and events, and the pictures will be talked about and we may well have to make explanations, but reading the story is the essence of this experience. Parents have not only prepared the way for this with the previous books, they have also told stories orally, not least about when they were children – and when they were naughty. But now it is the primacy of print which we wish to establish. Some experimentation may well be necessary to find out which stories really appeal, and it is advisable to start with short books until we can be sure interest will be sustained. Bumper books of a thousand famous fairy tales are all very well, but are heavy to hold and may not appeal. With such a great choice today parents can sometimes be put off and not know whether to choose a classic tale or the latest hyped cult craze. Advice from the children's librarian will help to narrow the field, but many parents have pointed out to us that they still want to find books to buy and keep because they know how much children enjoy hearing them being read over and over again.

Fairy tales, folk tales, myths, legends and children's classics abound, not to mention new and exciting tales which, each year, establish themselves as firm favourites. Because the choice is so great, the delights so many and varied, and because this is such an important formative time for our children, our advice is, go for old, go for good and go for gold. This is how and why we would set our sights high and duck the dross.

CHOOSING STORY BOOKS

* The more you like them, the better – you'll put them across!

* The older the tales, the better. The longer they've lasted the more likely they are to be of wide appeal and chime with children's imaginations.

* The better known they are, the better. Many of these tales are part of our language and culture – Cinderella, Jack the Giant Killer, Sinbad, Noah, Icarus – and need to be known.

* The more exciting they are, the better. Through the vicarious experience of stories children learn the eternal virtues and vices – courage and cowardice, faithfulness and betrayal, honesty and falsehood, love and hate, life and death.

* The shorter they are, the better. It is best to begin with a story one can finish in one short session. And there are so many tales to tell.

* The better written they are for reading aloud, the better. Beware long, complex sentences and go for variety of sentence length and crispness of style.

* Look for illustrations that add to the atmosphere and fill in the setting of the story; do the heroes and heroines appeal or repel? Short, re-told tales and most myths, legends and fables have few descriptions and leave a lot to the imagination, hence their appeal, but children will be helped in the early stages if the pictures cue them in.

* Go for value for money. Most major reputable publishers can keep costs down on these perennials and there are many paperbacks and facsimile versions around.

Most parents read to their children in bed and, of course, this is prime story time. For busy, active children, it is a good idea to read to them, if at all possible, before their day-time nap. Often parents find this promise of a story gets them settled quickly and avoids conflict. Parents enjoy the quietness, too! But, if it has not happened already, now is the time to make sure our children are really hooked on books. Now, too, they are going to be imprinted with print. Although we may be reading Pat Hutchins's *Rosie's Walk* or Dorothy Edwards's *My Naughty Little Sister* or a tale of Paddington Bear, we will be making it quite clear that we are following the line of the text, running our finger along under it, or turning the page and beginning by saying, 'I wonder what it says here?'

Some parents tend to slow down when they first start running their fingers under the text. The secret is to read with as much dramatic expression as is appropriate to the tale and make the finger keep pace with the voice. Don't make the mistake of trying to point to each word as it is said. The finger should move along under the *sentence* as it is read.

Most parents get a big kick out of these story-reading sessions, especially when they move on to the more dramatic tales. Maybe they bring out our hidden dramatic abilities. For those parents who find it difficult to throw their voices about, we have every sympathy. They should relax, let the stories speak for themselves and remember they have the most appreciative audiences in the world. If they can just act a little, it will help their children to understand and enjoy the stories.

By reading silently a sentence or two at a time and then saying what we have read, we are acting the part of the story-teller. Then, when the speech of the characters is introduced, we can try to act their parts. The fact that our children see us look and point at the text, perhaps pause and think before reading and occasionally use expressions such as, 'Let's find out what happens next!' or 'Let's see what it says!' demonstrate that reading is a purposeful, participatory activity from which we expect to get sense and meaning. If our children learn that, and in addition get all the enjoyment of the stories, they will never be like those children who build up the sounds of letters and make nonsense.

We believe that the story-telling which begins on the lap and carries on at nap time or reading time and at bed time, should continue for as long as children enjoy it. This may be long after they have learned to read for themselves. Certainly, children in school enjoy being read to and the experience is as valuable for them as it is for students at university to hear primary sources read by their lecturers. Helped by librarians, reviews and specialist journals about children's books, or guided by their children's interests and own good sense, parents can play a major part in introducing their children to language and literature in all their richness and diversity.

Many children enjoy discs and cassettes of stories recorded by professional actors and actresses to which they listen whilst following the texts in the accompanying books. These have a part to play but should be regarded as additions to, rather than replacements for, the parents' reading. The reason is plain: they are passive and non-interactive. Their big advantage is that they enable children to listen to language being read by a wider range of voices in a greater variety of accents. This helps children to become more aware of language, more conscious of the forms, registers, dialects and diversity of language.

The dangers of passive listening, without opportunities to ask questions and clarify points of confusion or ambiguity, are illustrated by the boy who thought that Mary's little lamb had fleas as white as snow, and by the girl who didn't want to hear a story called 'Jack and the Bean's Talk'. What makes lap learning in the early years so valuable is that the children feel secure and protected, cared for and the focus of attention, and that they are sharing in a mutually enjoyable activity in which they can learn. It is this, combined with the spell-binding magic of stories, which makes being read to so richly rewarding. It is this which is imprinting the children with print and associating books with pleasure. It is the natural context, therefore, in which to learn to read and the next stage takes them a step further along the way. Before we take that step, however, it is worthwhile to examine what parents have taught their children about reading so far.

WHAT PARENTS TEACH ABOUT READING BY ABOUT 3 YEARS OF AGE

* Books give pleasure.
* People and things can be shown in pictures.
* Pictures can be read and talked about.
* Pictures can both illustrate and tell stories.

* Books, their pictures, rhymes and stories can be talked about.
* Language in books is more particular and exact than it often is in speech.
* Language uses lots of little words to link and relate the words in sentences.
* Stories in books are about people and events which are somehow connected – they are about when or why or how things happen.
* Books contain rhymes and tales already known.
* Print is language which can be read. It tells tales and describes people and things.
* Being read to is enjoyable. The language is in lines of black letters of the alphabet which make up words.
* Print makes sense when followed from left to right.

As the children grow older, and heavier, lap learning is increasingly replaced by side-by-side learning. The intimate, interactive and warm relationship is as vital as ever. Reading and playing the language game remain the focus of concern, but now the children will increasingly take a more active part in reading.

6

How Parents Teach Reading – Side by Side

The success of lap learning and the happy introduction of story books is the bedrock on which the next phase of shared and paired reading rests. Children who have missed this introduction to books can be given it now, but parents should first make sure that the children enjoy looking at books with them and enjoy being read to. This means making sure that, no matter how old the children are, we respect their maturity and integrity by selecting books to look at and to read which are well within their ability to understand and, yet, which reflect their interests without appearing too babyish.

Now it is important to try, if at all possible, to select the best position to develop good study habits, on the lines set out on page 43. With these factors attended to, plus the children's enthusiastic enjoyment of being read to, we have established a good 'learning set', or predisposition to learning. If the enjoyment of story books with pictures has been continued long enough to have included books in which the pictures are smaller and less frequent, and in which the text has been getting longer, with the result that the stories have themselves been getting more important, it may be advisable to drop back to rather easier and shorter books first. The reason for this is that we want shared reading to be successful from the start. If parents decide that children would like to stay with the book, or the kind of book, they have already been reading, care should be exercised to ensure that they will have no difficulty with the new tasks.

Often the ideal book is one which has been read many times, a favourite which is virtually known by heart. This will be fine for establishing confidence and can be followed by slightly more demanding books. What is needed is a book parent and child can thoroughly enjoy together. Now, preferably in the appointed place, sitting side by side, a start can be made with shared reading.

Shared Reading

Having introduced the book, talked about the subject, place and characters, and answered the children's questions, the parent reads the story in the usual way, running a finger under the lines of print. Once the child is thoroughly absorbed in the story and is clearly enjoying it, the parent may safely assume that shared reading may begin. All that this involves is that, from time to time, when the parent is quite convinced the child will be able to give the correct response, there is a brief pause in which the child provides the next word or brief phrase. This may well be done, naturally, at the foot of a page, if the sentence runs on, or by saying in advance words to the effect that, 'We're going to play a little game. When I stop reading, you say what you think comes next!' As this is so much like the game all parents have played when they paused in singing a nursery rhyme, for the children to complete the line, most parents find it is a simple matter to get this going.

If there is the least hesitation or the children give the wrong word, the parents supply the correct answer without criticism, but with a brief hug. The hug, or a quick comment, such as 'Good' or 'Fine', is for the children's attempt, whether right or wrong. The right answer is any word which completes the sense of the sentence appropriately according to the context of the story. So, if the parent reads 'Ulysses and his crew climbed up the . . .' and the child says, 'mountain' but the book says, 'rocky slope', the parent simply says, 'Yes, it says "the rocky slope"' and carries on. However, had the child said, for example, 'tree' or 'because' then this is a clear indication that attention has been wandering, or that the story is not being understood. But this is a deliberate exaggeration of the sort of difficulty which could arise. Parents have little difficulty in deciding where to stop in the certainty that the children will supply the correct word.

From time to time, preferably at the beginning and just before the end of a session, it helps to take the children's hands and let them point their fingers along the line of print for a while as we read, or encourage them to watch our fingers and to 'follow the story'.

The Aim of Shared Reading

In shared reading, the aim is not to have the children following the text closely with their fingers or eyes all the time; it is to encourage them to attend to the text and to become familiar with scanning it from left to right, so that the association between print and language is firmly established. For this reason, parents occasionally pause in their reading to ask, 'What do you think happens next?' or 'Who do you think will . . .?' In other words, they ask questions which encourage the children to think about the story and the way it is developing. They will also ask questions about why the children think certain things happened in the story or whether they like or dislike certain characters.

Without excessive delay in the flow of the story, shared reading attempts to make the activity of reading as participatory as it can. If books are chosen which are readily finished in a few short sessions, the first session may be devoted to introducing the book and its characters, followed by uninterrupted reading to get well into the story. The second session could then begin with a brief check on how much is recalled of the story so far and the children's suggestions about what they think may happen next. The reading might then begin with the children following the text with their hand being led by ours and a couple of opportunities to guess the next word. In the final session, the introductory activities might include, for those children already able to write some of their letters, a Treasure Hunt for words beginning with letters they know.

Providing the interest of the children is maintained in the reading of the story, parents have no difficulty in directing attention to the print in these and other simple ways which are in harmony with the children's abilities. If there is any risk that the activities detract from the enjoyment of the reading sessions, then they should be dropped. Shared-reading activities can then be developed around the incidental reading of print in the home and elsewhere, whenever the opportunity arises. All that matters is that the children realize that print gives meaning and guessing gives sense, that beyond the print and the parent's voice, they are taking part in and enjoying the story. If they are now beginning to realize that reading is an activity in which they, too, can participate, then shared reading will have served its purpose.

In Appendix 7 and on pages 96–100, there are listed other activities and games which parents may like to incorporate into shared-reading sessions. If the children enjoy them and parents can spare a few minutes each day, these activities can be used with the books which the children have already heard read and have enjoyed. This often gives a new lease of life to the books and provides opportunities for games in which, as the books are so well known, there is no chance of being wrong and every opportunity to be right.

Reading Ready

Shared reading is a transitional stage to independent reading, and it is now that parents begin to wonder if their children want to learn to read. Some children by now will have already learnt to read, others will have made it quite clear that they want to learn. There is no reason to hurry the process along and no reason for anxiety if children are enjoying books, being read to, and are developing in the understanding and use of language. What parents can begin to look for are signs that children want to learn to read.

TEACH-ME-TO-READ SIGNS

* Enjoys being read to.
* Looks at books independently.
* Asks questions about books.
* Asks 'What does that say?' about print in books and in the environment; recognizes common signs.
* Wants to write own name or can already write it.
* Wants to put titles under drawings, paintings; traces/copies them.
* Recognizes some letters and some words.
* Enjoys shared reading – guesses what's next, follows text.
* Talks fluently and discusses present, recent past and planned events.

These are simply some of the signs to be on the alert for and there is no suggestion that all these signs have to be present. When a child announces, 'It says you've got to cut on the dotted line', or another asks, 'That says Hospital – what does that sign say?' pointing to an

Accident or Emergencies sign, then it is usually clear that they are already on the way to reading. They know that locked away in the print is a message and they have some of the keys to get to it.

It doesn't follow that, just because a child is lively and talkative, enjoys being read to, and is trying to copy letters, he wants to be taught to read or is even ready to learn. Just as some children seem to be on the point of walking for months, so some take longer than others to get round to wanting to learn to read. They may even see being able to read as something of a threat to the pleasure of being read to. Nor does it follow that the child of very few words is necessarily lagging behind and not eager to read. Some children, mercifully, are not garrulous. They may be thoughtful and reflective, weighing everything up very carefully and, only when they are sure of success, venturing to show what they can do. For all children, in all their glorious diversity, it is essential that there are plenty of books around for them to look at when they feel like it. If there's a space somewhere where all the books they have ever had, from their first rag or board book, can be kept together with their current library books and their bedtime and shared-reading books, so much the better. It may well be that amongst them they will one day find, to their and our delight and surprise, that there is a book that they can read.

Parents who have used techniques similar to those described as shared reading, whether their children have started reading or not, know that a lot more support and encouragement is needed. The child who happily reads, 'But, Grandma, what big eyes you've got!' may turn to a newspaper and fail to recognize anything which makes sense. Getting children launched into reading, so that they can begin to read anything appropriate to their age and experience, need not wait until they start school. Paired reading provides the support and accelerates progress.

Paired Reading

Paired reading is to reading what supporting children on their bikes is to cycling. We first saw paired reading being used with deaf children some twenty years ago and were so impressed that we tried it out with children teaching children. That experience, incidentally, gave us the confidence to suggest to some parents of large families that the eldest might well teach the youngest. Subsequently, as described earlier, we have used paired reading with all ages and abilities. In our action research project in Wales, the parents called it 'unison reading' which, with the Welsh love of unison singing, seemed appropriate. Other names for the techniques are 'read along' and 'reading together' although we have a preference for what one boy called it, 'two-headed reading' – it is certainly better than one! Many parents just say, 'Now you read with me', and that is enough to start the process going. It follows on quite naturally from shared reading.

The essence of the paired-reading technique is that parent and child read together, just as they might sing together, while the parent runs a finger under the line of print. As with teaching a child to ride a bike, the parent gets the child going confidently and then, imperceptibly, briefly releases the bike for a moment, so, when the child is reading confidently, the parent may pause for the child to say the next word and then continue reading together. This is the essence of the method and often this is enough to get children started. Unfortunately, it is rather hit or miss, and, with a skill as important as reading, it is essential to have a technique which has inbuilt fail-safe procedures and guarantees success in the vast majority of cases. *At this stage the objective is to enable the child to become an independent reader without experiencing failure. If the system we recommend is followed, and if the children are succeeding in the reading and writing activities described in this and the next chapter, no matter how long the process may take, there is no risk of the child being exposed to failure. Children and parents who read together, succeed together.*

Beginning Paired Reading

The technique begins with the selection of a suitable book which interests the child, and which will be thoroughly enjoyed and understood. If it has been read before and will be enjoyed again, then it may well serve as an ideal introduction. Usually, however, it helps to start with a new and exciting book to give the proceedings a sense of occasion and high purpose. Anything which boosts the children's egos and helps them to feel that they are going to have some fun with us will help to make a good start. So, an enthusiastic parent waving a book and saying, 'Let's have a read together!' is all that most children need if the right time and place have been chosen. If it is a new book, the parents should have familiarized themselves with it in advance. It is also advisable to check, in advance, how many pages one can comfortably read, with plenty of expression, in one minute. In the early stages it is strongly urged that sessions are short. Once the system is working successfully the time can be increased a little at a time. Don't be tempted, however, if the first sessions go swimmingly, to double the time – this is as dangerous as doubling the dosage of medicines just because they work! The essential ingredient of all fun is the timing. Here is an outline of the system. It is fun which works.

PAIRED-READING TECHNIQUE

1. Brief introduction to the book, its characters, pictures. Parent says, 'First, I'll read – you follow the story as I read it to you', or similarly. About 1 minute.

2. Parent reads, with expression, at normal pace whilst running finger under the print. About 1 minute.

3. Parent answers any questions about story so far, explains any possible difficult points, briefly, and says, in effect, 'Now you read it with me and let's see how we go!' They read together the same passage as before, parent again running finger under print. About 1 minute.

4. Parent praises child for reading so well. Says, 'Let's try that again. It sounds as if you can read it as well as me!' They read together the same passage as before, parent running finger under print. This time parent pauses a couple of times for child to provide the next word or phrase at a point at which child is most likely to be correct. If child hesitates or makes mistakes, parent supplies the correct word and they carry on together.

5. Parent praises child for reading so well and for having a shot at supplying the next word. Parent says, 'This time I'll start you off,

then you carry on reading.' Parent and child read first few words and child carries on reading with occasional 'goods' or prompts if needed from parent. If necessary, parent resumes reading with child to keep natural pace going.

6. Parent praises the child for trying and for reading so well.

What, of course, we've not been able to put in are the hugs, smiles and exclamations of delight provided as an appropriate accompaniment by the parent as the child reads! It is essential that, whatever happens, the child is praised. Should the child freeze on being asked to carry on and be clearly unable to do so, then we need only praise the attempt and blame ourselves for choosing the wrong book or the wrong time. Shared reading can then be resumed and the session end in success. To recapitulate, the sequence of paired reading, after the preliminaries, is:

PAIRED-READING SEQUENCE

1. Introduction.
2. Parent reads passage for 1 minute.
3. Parent and child read same passage as before for 1 minute.
4. Parent and child read same passage with parent pausing for child to supply next word a couple of times. 1 minute.
5. Child reads same passage aloud alone, parent supporting if necessary. 1 minute.
6. Parent praises.

The words put into our imaginary parent's mouth are only intended to suggest the instruction, not the actual words to be used. Most parents build up a repertoire of instructions and prompts during their shared-reading sessions, quite apart from during all their other activities together. The more natural and appropriate the instructions can be, the better. We also believe that it helps many children to know that their parents are now going to set about teaching them to read. If this is seen as the welcome beginning of a successful adventure, fine. If it is seen as a threat, then it will be counterproductive and best avoided. On the other hand, some children at this stage are so practical and serious that they will be put off if their parents suggest they are going to play a new and exciting *game*. They prefer everything to be 'for real'. Other children need coaxing. Some treat everything as a great joke. Whatever the case, the name of the game is *reading* and it is about this that we wish to enthuse them.

For most children the new elements in paired reading will be the reading together and reading on their own. It often happens that on the first couple of occasions the novelty of the situation detracts from their concentration on the reading. If this is the case, continue reading together for as long as you think appropriate. Never allow children to flounder and never tell them a word is wrong in these early days. It is always better to tell them the correct word and move on. Again, some children take a few sessions to get into their stride when reading together. If it is thought necessary to slow down for them, try to build the pace up a little each time in subsequent sessions. What matters is that the sense and expression are preserved.

Every opportunity should be taken to praise the children in paired-reading sessions. This will focus attention on the things they are doing well and shape their behaviour towards reading. We can praise them for listening, following the print, trying, sitting quietly and attentively, for speaking clearly, giving the right word, concentrating, guessing, reading on their own, reading with expression, reading so many words or for being able to read, or for whatever they have done. Some parents have found that concentrating on things to praise has helped them to realize that sometimes, especially when older children complain of parents 'picking on them', criticism and correction make things worse. Praise helps children to feel confident and successful and fuels their motivation to persevere with tasks. We want them to feel successful readers from the start so that whatever little difficulties they may encounter will be seen as problems with the task itself and not as failures or deficiencies in themselves.

Fortunately, parents more often than not adopt a different teaching strategy from teachers when things go wrong and children encounter difficulties. Teachers often first blame the method and then the child. Parents tend to blame themselves first, then the method and, last of all, the child. This is because, as parents, we expect to be continuously making changes and adjustments in order to meet our children's needs. We see our children as active learners who are eager to succeed and our role as that of helping them to do so. In using the paired-reading technique we have found the majority of parents quickly adopt a sensible and successful strategy which gets their children learning to read by reading. From now on, most of the problems encountered will be dealt with by the on-task activities described below, at the end of the paired-reading sessions, or in the write-and-spell and other Language Experience activities. They will be dealt with as and when they arise and most will be quickly despatched.

What is important to recognize now is that both paired reading and reading to the children at bedtime or during the day should be continued until they are reading successfully on their own. Even then, paired reading will be found useful from time to time, when difficult texts are encountered, and many children can be helped to discover new delights or new interests if we introduce them to particular books by reading from them. Don't adults listen to *A Book at Bedtime* and other radio and TV book programmes, or find that a film or TV series will awaken interest in books and authors? Having taught our children to read is no mean achievement, but teaching them to read successfully is to teach them so that they go on reading. Paired reading is completely free of stress or anxiety and, so far as the children are concerned, successful. If we have introduced it too soon then nothing is lost because we can revert to shared reading until such time as we consider it prudent to try again. Some parents, when they have been introduced to the technique have said, 'Surely, all the children are doing is learning what to say by heart – that's not reading, it's memorizing!' In part, they are right. Where they are wrong is in failing to recognize what a major part memory plays in reading. Paired reading works for a number of reasons which we discussed in Chapter 3. We summarize them here.

WHY PAIRED READING WORKS

* The message is understood before it is read.
* Print is used as a prompt to memory.
* The reader only uses those cues necessary.
* Scanning is automatized and can focus on meaning.
* Reader is secure and supported by parent.
* The task is self-rewarding and also rewarded by parent's praise.
* It's learning to read by reading and getting it all together.

But reading aloud is not silent reading, and reading with support is not independent reading. As the child progresses, the sessions may gradually be lengthened, as suggested earlier. It is also possible to accelerate progress, should the child appear to be ready, by introducing texts of greater difficulty. Advances may be made a little at a time, to avoid the risk of failure, but we should be guided by the child's ability to understand. The sight of a 5-year-old reading *The Financial Times*, Dickens or *Lorna Doone*, without understanding, is as distressing as seeing a monkey in clothes. If children are enjoying and understanding what they read – *at their level* – then they are truly print-borne.

From time to time in paired reading, children may experience difficulties with specific letters, letter strings or words. Some of these little problems can be dealt with when they are learning to write and spell, but many can be dealt with, as and when they arise, at the end of the paired-reading session. Alternatively, they can be left until time allows, together with the paired-reading book and, ideally, in the spot selected for working together. The games suggested here and in Appendix 7 need a light touch when they are introduced and there is no reason why the children should regard them as anything but games. The last thing we want to suggest is that the children should think of them as punitive exercises or work. Children's play *is* hard work and, if happily involved, as all parents know, they will persist and give it their undivided attention.

One problem that some parents are concerned about at this stage is their children's speech. Some are concerned about local accents, some about correcting slovenly speech, whilst others notice that the children are 'falling over themselves' when they speak, are breathless or have difficulty with certain sounds. Serious speech difficulties should, of course, receive early specialist diagnosis and therapy. Here we are concerned only with those minor problems parents may encounter which are well within their competence to solve. Primarily, our main concern is with making the most of paired reading.

Talking Tall

When children read aloud with and to us, we want them to do so with confidence and clarity. We don't want them to shout, be strident, squeak or be overassertive any more than we want them to mumble, stumble or bumble. But, telling a child to speak up is a put-down. If we say, 'Stop mumbling!' it's a shut-up. The strategies we suggest for all problems of this order, which strike at the heart of the children's self-concepts and self-confidence, are, firstly, good example and, secondly, talking tall.

From the beginning, we have emphasized the importance of reading to children with plenty of expression and at a natural pace. The first aspect of being a good example, therefore, is to make sure that we are reading clearly and giving full value to the beginning and ends of words. Clear articulation and expressive speech is good speech, whatever the regional accent. But the other side of the coin is being a good example, is being an attentive listener. With most children at some time in these early years, we need to show children *how we hear them.* There is one way which parents will already be familiar with, it is like marital deafness, and we call it parental deafness! These forms of deafness are forms of acting: we heard but act as if we hadn't. So, instead of telling children to speak up or to stop talking through their beards, we simply say, 'Sorry, I didn't hear that. What did you say?' Similarly, to the children who run their words together or subvocalize, we can help them by blaming ourselves for not having heard. What we must remember is that, as parents, we are so used to being LASSes and virtually interpreting our children's speech, often knowing what they are trying to say before they have thought of it, that we are now having to reverse the process. Now we are understanding the child but recognizing that others might not be able to. Paired reading, by drawing our attention to the child's speech, provides an excellent opportunity for encouraging good speech. One of the characteristics we want to develop, above all others, is self-confidence. When children are with other children, at play school or ordinary school, with visitors or visiting, or just out and about, we want them to speak with confidence, look at people when they are talking, and express themselves appropriately. We want them to be good companions *and* good communicators.

We also want them to become increasingly aware of language so that, as they develop, they will think about what they say, about what people or print mean, and about how language is used. Being language-conscious or language-alive is important at this stage for our children because now they are meeting it in print and reading it aloud. The more alive they are to the importance of speaking clearly, the more alert they will be to the little words and to the beginnings, middles and ends of all words. Language begins by clothing and articulating thought, and develops through usage and through thinking. So far as our children are concerned, we want them to become increasingly alert to the patterns of sounds and of letters as they speak, read and write. We want natural speech clearly articulated. We will get this by encouraging our children to talk tall.

ENCOURAGING CHILDREN TO TALK TALL

* Encourage good posture with head up and slightly back at all times and especially when speaking.
* Standing or seated, if good posture is not natural, encourage the feeling that they are dangling, like puppets on a string, from the tops of their heads.
* Encourage looking at people when speaking to them and looking up when reading aloud.
* Encourage speaking out with clear articulation which gives full value to the syllables, their stress, and the sounds of natural speech.
* Encourage reading silently ahead before looking up and saying what was read.
* Achieve confident, pleasant, clear reading and communication by commenting favourably on upright posture, good eye contact, clear diction, pleasant tone of voice, etc.; by giving a good model and commenting favourably on others' speech (not other children's); and by feigning parental deafness.

In Britain, much more than in many parts of the USA, speech is a major mark of the social strata to which people are assigned or assign themselves. As we move towards the twenty-first century, there will be increasing demands for participatory democracy, access to information, social mobility, good communicators, and the superficial, but divisive, trappings of social class and stratification will mean less and less. If we bring up all our children talking tall there will be fewer people around to talk up or down to.

* We need confident, clear speech as a natural behaviour, like upright posture – in contrast to grunts and stooped posture.
* Neurologically and psychologically we function better in upright, confident postures.
* We want to encourage communication.
* We want language aliveness.
* We want the patterns of speech and of print to be heard and seen in the context of language.
* We want nothing to stand between language and meaning, whether language is spoken, heard, printed or being written.
* We want language established in our children as the natural way of expression, more potent than physical force, more persuasive than coercion and more authoritative than violence or the exercise of power.
* Talking tall means I am what I say, what I say I mean, and what I mean I do.
* Talking tall is the social communicating act of according respect and regard for one's listeners.
* Talking tall is giving oneself the dignity of self-respect.

There is ample evidence that encouraging children to talk tall helps to improve their reading and their spelling and, whilst these are our main concerns in this context we cannot ignore the broader social dimensions. It has long been part of educational mythology that socially disadvantaged children were additionally handicapped by defective language, and only in the past decade or so is this 'non-science' being blown away. What disadvantages children is what disadvantages their families which, in very many cases, is their hopelessness and helplessness and absence of power or control over their futures. This can only drive them into apathy or violence. What is depressing is to witness what was called the cycle of poverty, or disadvantage, as generation after generation sinks further and further behind the rest of society. This has nothing to do with people's vocabulary or syntax or their abilities. It is the result of many historical, social and economic factors of which greed and aggression are common components. What is inspiring is when education, often self-education, enables people to express their thoughts and demands and break out of the poverty trap. In teaching our children to read we should not ignore the potential of universal literacy, inadequate though the levels may be, in its ability to transform societies. We are educating our children to equip them for their own futures – they will be better able to do this if they talk tall. They will be able to spell better, too!

Games to Go with Paired Reading

When we find that children are having difficulties with specific words, letter strings or letters, one of the easiest games to play is **Hunt the . . .** If the trouble has been, say, mixing *is* with *as*, we can focus attention on discriminating between them by playing 'Hunt the *a*s' or 'Hunt the letter *a*'. Now the child simply goes back over the passage pointing out all the *a*s. This can be followed by, 'Hunt the *as*' – looking this time for the word *as*. Concentrating upon the *a* and ignoring the *i* is usually enough to develop discrimination. If we try, in the same session, treating the *i* in this way, we may only cause greater confusion.

Once a game like this is established, it can be varied and increased in the fun it gives either by counting the number the child finds or by setting a time limit in which to find, say, ten. Don't expect the children to hunt and count, however, as they will find this almost impossible to do; the objective is that they concentrate on looking for the letter, letter string or word.

When the children are able to write, of course, the **Hunt** games can be modified so that they are now told to 'Hunt out and write down all the words beginning with *st* . . . or ending with . . . *gh*', for example. Now, the focus of attention upon a specific word or letter string is reinforced by the act of writing them down a number of times.

Another way of focusing attention upon letter and word patterns is to play **I Spy a word beginning with** . . . Here, parents may use either the sound or the name of letters, focusing attention upon whichever aspect may help the child at the time. Only a quick glance will be needed to make sure that, in a passage already read a number of times, suitable words exist to exercise and strengthen the child's ability. Thus, a child who is unsure of the letter *b* might be told the sound of the letter, to avoid confusion with the letter *d*, whilst a child who is having difficulty with recognizing a particular word might be given its initial letter's name. Variations of I Spy, using the text of the paired-reading passage, are **I Spy a word ending in . . .** and **I Spy a word with . . . in it**. In this way the beginnings, ends and middles of words can become the focus of attention. Letter strings, such as *wh-*, *ch-*, *sh-*, *spr-*, *fl-* at the beginnings, *-ing*, *-ion*, *-th*, *-ch*, *-nd* at the ends, and *-tt-*, *-ll-*, *-ea-*, *-ou-*, *-ee-* in the middle, may be used. They are listed, with examples, in Appendix 5.

One of the important aspects of reading for meaning is our ability to recognize whole syllables. In countries with phonetically consistent alphabets, where all words are spelt as they sound, children still have to know how to break words up into syllables and which syllables to stress, or otherwise, in reading. In English we have a number of syllables which have meanings, the prefixes and suffixes, such as *bi-*, *dis-*, *non-*, *poly-*, *un-* and *-ant*, *-ent*, *-ing*, *-ian*, *-ology*, *-ly* and *-ed*, and are therefore particularly important. We can hunt or spy for these but, as this search requires more than simple recognition, parents may prefer to call these **Find me** games. A brief preliminary explanation, pointing out the syllable and its meaning, if it has one, can be followed by the instruction **Find me the syllable 'per'** or **Find me a syllable that means 'not'**.

Find me games can be extended to cover word meanings. When children start to read and to become skilled in the use of language, they demonstrate their interest in meaning by their fascination with riddles, conundrums and jokes, especially punning jokes. So playing games of **Find me a word that means . . .** will set them off searching happily. Again, **Find me a word that is the opposite of . . .** may be played. Another aspect of words which children find fascinating is their rhyming. **Find me a word that rhymes with . . .** might be used to familiarize a child with a word which caused difficulty and point up its similarity with better known words. **Find me the words that tell us . . .** or **Find me the sentence which tells us . . .** are instructions for searches which draw attention to the meaning of the texts. Here we may use the same words or our own words for those in the book.

Counting games, if the children are fairly secure with numbers and counting up to, say, twenty, are also popular and can direct attention to important aspects of the passage. **Count the sentences/ full stops/capital letters/paragraphs/colours/characters/animals** etc. are just a few of the counting games. Later, it is always an interestinggame to find the most common letters – and the least common ones, too – by getting the children to count the *e*s, say, in a sample of lines. Some children will then want to make counts of all the letters and keep records of them. These counting games help children to recognize that there are 'families' of things, they introduce them to key concepts, such as sentences or punctuation marks, and also demonstrate that we count the members of sets of things with common characteristics.

What's in the Window? is another on-task game which helps children to become familiar with the patterns of print and the common strings of letters. To play this, a piece of card or a postcard is required. Around the edge and from the middle of the card, windows of different sizes are cut, as in this example. The actual sizes of window will depend on the size of print in the book being read, although one does not need to be too fussy about this, providing the windows are big enough to isolate syllables and words of different length. Another card can be used to place under a line of print when it is wished to draw attention to it but with this card the purpose is to isolate the beginnings, middles and ends of words or whole words.

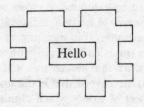

In playing all these games, and those included in the Language Experience activities section and Appendix 7, begin by setting tasks which the children are sure to be able to get right and only introduce the more difficult tasks, which will be the ones we may wish to teach or exercise, gradually. *All the games should be short, sharp bursts of fun*

occupying little more than a minute at the most. They must always enable the children to show us what they know and what they can do.

Anagrams are helpful in drawing attention to letters in words with which the children may have had difficulty. Once children have been shown that the letters of a word can be reassembled to make another word or words, they will enjoy playing with them and begin to notice them. So, although not all words lend themselves to apt anagrams, such as *train – it ran* or *panties – a step-in*, we can let the children have what fun they can simply by saying, **How many words can you make with . . .?** If we choose a word in which we can see one or two smaller words, the chances are there will be more to be found. Perhaps, in the process they will discover an anagram they recognize. For example, *result – rest, use, user, set, let, rule, Sue, rust, rustle.* A useful tip, which will help children, is to include *the* or *a* with the word you wish them to use, if it is a noun, or to make the word a part of a short phrase. In this way they will be able to make many more words. Making words from other words helps with spelling, develops awareness of language, increases active, as opposed to passive, vocabulary and is fun.

Codes provide another game, which children enjoy playing, which has the advantage of focusing attention on the individual letters of words. As we discovered with the dyslexic pupils, who, according to research, have such difficulty with decoding, they not only enjoyed doing them, but some felt they helped more than anything else to break the code of print. Of course, codes should only be used if children enjoy doing them but a great deal depends upon how they are introduced. If the first message they decipher is, 'I love you!' or 'Surprise for you in the cupboard', they may be more receptive to the idea of using codes than if their introduction to them is associated with spelling mistakes! Children who are beginning to read well but who stumble over unfamiliar words and have difficulty in remembering spelling will enjoy exchanging messages about activities with parents, siblings and friends. All that is necessary is to provide a simple substitution number code such as this:

A	B	C	D	E	F	G	H	I	J	K	L	M
2	3	5	7	11	13	17	19	23	1	4	6	8

N	O	P	Q	R	S	T	U	V	W	X	Y	Z
9	10	12	14	15	16	18	20	26	21	22	25	24

Start with a number code because an alphabet code can be confusing with young children. Thus, START = 16 18 2 15 18, and 16 18 10 12 = STOP. Always leave larger spaces between the figures than is usual and make clear gaps or strokes / between words.

It is a simple matter to change the code by changing the numbers and, once the children become proficient, alphabetic substitution codes may be introduced such as this:

a b c d e f g h i j k l m n o p q r s t u v w x y z

P L M N K O B J W U H V C G Y T D X R E Z S A Q F I

The alphabet, in clear, has been written in lower-case letters to help the children distinguish it from the code in capitals. Now *start* = REPXE. Later other ciphers, such as Playfair, may be introduced for variety with older children. Although, like anagrams, codes draw attention to individual letters and may be used to help children overcome spelling difficulties, it is important to remember that words are best learned in a context and, for this reason, it is better to move quickly from writing individual words in code to writing simple sentences incorporating the words on which attention is being focused. One by-product of playing with codes is that some children will realize that the patterns of letters in print are revealed by the patterns in the codes. Children begin by noticing how often E or its substitute appears. They notice that a single-letter word is likely to be *a* or *I* and a frequently recurring three-letter word may be *the*.

Once they begin noticing these frequency patterns, or realize they are there when they have been pointed out, they can be given, not the full alphabet, but a single word in a code, for example, ESPIONAGE = LKIBGTDXL, as their only cue to a coded message containing a fair proportion of the letters in the code word, and encouraged to guess the rest. For instance, XG VG KIDBT = GO TO SPAIN. Children with a mathematical bent or who become interested in these codes, we have found, can be helped in this way to take a new interest in print and language, subjects they may previously have found difficult or antipathetic.

Memory

One problem which may be thrown up through the use of codes is that some children have difficulties in remembering. Primary memory difficulties will be shown by the inability to remember the substitution number or letter between looking it up and writing it down. Secondary, or long-term memory difficulties will *possibly* be involved in remembering the message or sentence once it has been read through after it has been decoded. In Appendix 7 we suggest some measures to help children's memories. We still know very little about how memory is stored biochemically in the brain, but we know more about its attributes and how it operates. From this it is clear that one way in which children may be helped to learn to read is by consciously learning to memorize. Young children don't consciously memorize and it is only around 8 or 9 years of age that children usually use methods such as repeating the name of whatever they may wish to memorize, unless they are frequently reminded to do so. Yet most children have phenomenal memories. In the early years they remember and use appropriately words they may have only encountered briefly. From 6 or 7 years of age, they have the ability to learn things by heart with remarkable ease. What we need to do to help them is to encourage them to remember those things which are most closely associated with reading. The ability to remember telephone numbers or the shapes of aeroplanes or birds is different from the facility to remember the words of pop songs or people's faces. We have found, not surprisingly, therefore, that children are most helped to read by consciously trying to memorize language in print.

Memory and Verse

Memory of memory is aided by seven (plus or minus two) Rs!

> Recognize
> Register
> Receive
> Relate
> Record
> Rehearse
> Retain
> Refresh
> Retrieve

Most of us can remember five to nine things at any one time. We are fortunately better able to forget than remember and usually need to recognize in order to register something. But having got it into memory store, there's the problem of retrieving it again. That's helped by hooking it on to other things already in store, by saying it over to retain it, reminding ourselves to refresh our memory and by recalling it. If we can remember something visually, orally, rhythmically, aurally and cognitively, then it will be better tagged for retrieval than if it has only been registered by one sense or faculty. Chanting tables rhythmically is better than saying them monotonously. Chanting them without understanding them will make it almost impossible to retrieve what we want to know when we need it. Chanting with understanding, whilst refreshing oneself with the sight of the patterns (9, 18, 27, 36 . . .), is of more value than passive prodding of pocket calculators, as all employers know. The language in print which is supported by rhythm and rhyme, alliteration and assonance, sense and the senses, is verse. For children, we choose comic and nonsense verse as best matched to their needs and most likely to amuse them. Not only does it follow on naturally from lap learning nursery rhymes, it also demonstrates the application of a law we discovered when working with severely physically handicapped children with gross communication problems. The law is: find a way to make a child smile and educate accordingly. Even when reduced to Yes/No gestures, for example, it is possible to make children laugh or smile by the novel or incongruous. With children blessed with language and all their senses we must first find the short verses which amuse them, tell them to learn them and see if they can.

The small anthology of comic and nonsense verse we compiled for the parents to use on our action research project consisted of profound pieces such as this:

> *Uncle did you feel no pain*
> *Falling from the apple tree?*
> *Will you do it, please, again –*
> *Cousin Willie didn't see.*

Parents, whose children found it difficult to learn the verses they liked, were encouraged to make sure they understood them, read them over as in paired reading, and then repeat them using the LCC technique. **Look, Cover** and **Check**, which can be applied to learning spellings or anything else, involves saying the verse over and over three or four times, with expression, whilst looking at it. The verse is then covered and the learner attempts to repeat it from memory. When the learner breaks down or gets to the end, the text is uncovered and checked. Look, Cover and Check is repeated until memorization is completed satisfactorily. If larger portions are to be learned they are broken down into four or five lines or groups. When this is done, the first group is learned again with the second group, the first and second groups relearned with the third group, and so on, to make sure that ultimately the chunks are all learned together as one whole. Chunking like this can be used with the children using the LCC technique on each line, but this should rarely be necessary.

Learning comic verse was so popular with some children that they urged their parents to buy books of verse to extend their repertoires. Many parents found that they remembered suitable verses, some made parodies of limericks and adapted them, others included clerihews and tongue-twisters. Many children were particularly helped by writing out the verses. This, of course, helped hand-writing, spelling and memorization. But again, it cannot be stressed too strongly, parents must be guided by their children to find what they think is funny. From that, all else may follow.

Although we have introduced these games and activities as particularly suitable for dealing with difficulties which may arise in paired reading, they are not intended as any more than that. Paired reading will get children print-borne and, in many cases, reading simple texts competently, but the write-and-spell and Language Experience activities, described in the following chapters, are designed to provide all children with access to all that they need to know about the encoding of language in print. Paired reading gets children print-borne because the parents provide support and the meaning of the message while the children read it. Write-and-spell and Language Experience start with the children's words and messages, and the parents provide the help and support to put them in print and writing.

The two lines of development, reading and writing, progress simultaneously and complement and supplement one another. Thus, they are developing hand in hand. At the same time, too, children will be learning from the print at home and in the world around them. Familiarity feeds facility.

From Lap Learning to Literacy – a Sketch Map

LEARNING TO READ BY READING

Conversation and playing the language game with our children, in everyday situations, develop their thinking and their understanding and use of language. This is the basis on which we can talk them into reading. In turn, once they can read, reading will further develop their thinking and language abilities.

9 months	Pointing at things
	Pointing at pictures
	Rag and board books
12 months	Picture books
	Picture story books
	Picture alphabet books
	Picture and word books
	Story books with pictures
3 years	Shared reading
	Shared-reading games
4 years	Paired reading
	Paired-reading games
6 years	Prepared reading – reading to learn
7 years	Guided reading
	Study methods
10 years	Independent study
	Discriminatory reading
	Critical reading

Starting ages

The ages indicate the *earliest* at which some children will want to take an active part in the various activities, but there will always be exceptions. The reverse is also true: enjoyment of books with pictures does not stop at infancy. The sequence merely indicates a progression from learning to read, to reading to learn. It is a sequence we may, in part, repeat when embarking on a new subject.

Reading ability

We never stop learning to read and the concept of a Reading Age is meaningless. The question we should ask about a child's or adult's reading ability is, 'What can they read?' In Appendix 8 we give simple tests of functional reading ability. In using these Criterion Reading Tests it is important to remember that it is the ability to understand the meaning of the texts or tasks which is assessed, not the mere ability to 'bark at print'.

7

'I Can Read What I Wrote'

Like the starting point for reading, the starting point for printing and writing is pointing. Most children demonstrate their finger-painting abilities with their food and progress from this, and the ability just to point at things, to holding a crayon and scribbling, if they are given the opportunity. If they are given the opportunity – is an important proviso. As the chart below demonstrates, we know that most children show a general sequence of development. It is usually assumed that this sequence is the result of the development of the nervous system from the cerebral cortex, or surface of the brain, and the spinal column outwards to the limbs. Different parts of the brain develop at different times and at different rates. Functions in the limbs are from gross to fine motor movements. Infancy is observably a period of enormously rapid cerebral and neural development. What we still don't fully understand is the extent to which this development is prompted by external stimulus and opportunity. We once thought that walking needed the opportunities that crawling, reaching up and exploring provide. But children who spend the first two years of their lives carried on their mothers' backs quickly learn to walk once they are allowed to do so and appear to have suffered no ill-effects from this 'developmental delay'. On the other hand, handicapped children without arms can develop dexterity with their feet. Babies, whose left side of the brain may have been damaged, can develop speech and language abilities, which are normally centred in the left side, in the right hemispheres of their brains. The brain not only has what we call plasticity, the ability to develop functions in areas not usually associated with them, but also the ability to respond to the demands made upon it. This appears to be particularly possible in infancy but also, with training, as in victims of poliomyelitis and other handicapping conditions, with older people. It also appears, from the work done in the Peto Institute in Hungary, and by therapists who use the Peto method

NB All ages are approximate; individual variations are great.

12 months	Handedness emerging. Can hold crayon in fist and scribbles. Points index finger. Finger paints.
15 months	Scribbles up and down – using full arm.
18 months	More extensive scribbling and from right to left.
21 months	Scribbles round and round.
24 months	May name scribble. Can copy a vertical stroke down the page. (Letter I.) Uses paints and brush.
27 months	Scribbling becomes increasingly purposeful. Paints. Copies horizontal stroke. (Letters T, L.)
30 months	Wrist movements developing. Finger hold of crayon or brush. Crude copy of circle. (Letters O, C.)
33 months	Imitative – with wrist and finger movements (fine motor) developing – can shade in areas. Copies a cross crudely. (Letters t, x.)
36 months	Begins holding pencil between finger and thumb. Draws crude picture of man, neckless, armless, some with head and feet. Can use scissors.
4 years	Copies a ladder shape. (Letters H, E, F.) Likes drawing human figure, head with eyes dotted in, arms may be added. Some children now copy name and can copy Mummy/Daddy – others make little attempt to copy letters.
5 years	Can draw square. Circle and cross now well formed. House drawn crudely, windows in corners. Stick man or figure with head, body, limbs, fingers. Beginning of printing letters.
6 years	Can draw what is known schematically. Many children can write full name, some are now printing and spelling, with help, what they want to say. Most children by the end of the year, can draw a man with head, arms and feet and over half now give a neck.
7 years	Copies a square clearly, and a ladder clearly. Copies a diamond for first time crudely. Triangle copied well. Some children now writing cursive, majority can print and should be able to write their own names in full. Faces can now be drawn in profile.

with children with cerebral palsy in this country and elsewhere, that development of physical abilities is facilitated by using speech. This is not so strange as it sounds.

We are all familiar, from our own experience, with the value of talking ourselves through a particularly tricky manoeuvre and know that, in learning skills, such as music and dance, crafts and athletics, counting or repeating the names of the steps in a sequence of operations is common practice. From watching our children, we know that they will often mutter to themselves as they attempt to perform tasks. This use of language is one we shall employ in the suggestions we make for teaching writing. Whether early stimulation and opportunity to develop skills before the ages at which they normally appear accelerates development, or simply taps latent abilities, no one at present knows. What is beyond doubt is that parental encouragement which leads normal development and gives children enjoyment is preferable to the under-estimation of children's abilities. Lack of stimulation results in boredom, incompetence and failure. Harmony with the child and that uncommon commodity, common sense, are what count in whatever we do.

The chart makes it clear that the children in these early years have two problems to overcome in graphical representation: their manual ability to control the crayon or pencil and their limited perceptual abilities. In the beginning, their drawings are what *they* say they are, no matter how they may appear to us. Although they may know they have arms and a neck they will not draw them. They are drawing images or icons of the real thing. Even when they develop fine finger control, and are thoroughly acquainted with reading pictures and watching television, they will not know how to use perspective and cars will be little more than boxes on wheels. Not surprisingly, therefore, their attempts at letter shapes lag behind their ability to copy crosses and circles in many cases. But, the range of abilities in children is very great and, in support of the suggestion that language may help the performance of tasks when children are given opportunity, some children are writing remarkably fluently although their ability to copy a triangle (A) or diamond ($\Diamond$ only a square rotated through 45°) is still rudimentary.

Neurologically, a significant development takes place at around 6 years of age. Our spatial abilities, involved in our perception of how things are placed in space and in our ability to think in 3D, develop on the right side of the brain. The development is usually earlier in boys than in girls who are in most respects, on average, in advance of boys. It is important for girls and boys to develop these abilities, whenever they come, in relation to their other abilities and here language may well have a role to play. We do not subscribe to the view put forward by some specialists that some boys, whose spatial abilities develop markedly earlier than girls, may be disadvantaged by having 'two right hemispheres and no left'. We do believe that if we are alert to our children's needs, we can usually remedy minor imbalances in development by simple means. Just as some children become left-handed by neglect, so others become confused about orientation and direction, and others become dyslexic. Children have the potential to become many things in their early years and parents who monitor their children's development with sensitivity, and provide plenty of stimuli and a variety of options, are best placed to guide their acquisition of skills in the most propitious directions. This is the case with learning to print and to write. Again, whenever children appear to be encountering difficulties, ask them what they find difficult – they may well be able to tell us. We may be able to tell them how to talk themselves through the task. For example, the child who had difficulty making the letter *a* was told simply, 'A for apple, on a stick – first the apple O, then the stick Q !' Given that example, and the suggestion that she should say those words whilst making the shape of the letter, was enough to correct the difficulty.

Painting to Print

Drawing, painting, modelling and playing with a wide variety of everyday materials are the best preparation for writing. Even before children are able to make letter shapes they can play with wooden and plastic cut outs of them. Having seen the letters in their ABC books, they can find and tear or cut out letters from newspapers and magazines. They can draw round shapes or stencils and become familiar with the shapes and their names. As we watch them growing in ability and in enjoying what they are doing, we can judge when it may be best to introduce printing. Children may be able to copy a few individual letters by around 2½ years of age but, as indicated in the development chart, the letters which may be written before 3 years of age are very few. We would be far better engaged in simply encouraging plenty of painting and drawing and watching for the appearance of circles, vertical and horizontal lines.

Somewhere between 2½ and 4 years of age a start can be made. Nothing is more important to children than their own names. It is tragic when one finds young people and adults who have been through the educational system but remain incapable of writing their own names. Yet most of them can be taught in precisely the same way as we suggest for young children. Whilst some children need showing once, the majority need much more help. We break the task down into three stages, each stage being mastered thoroughly before proceeding to the next. Note, we are only talking here about *copying* as preliminary to actually writing freely without a copy.

THREE-STAGE METHOD FOR TEACHING CHILDREN TO COPY THEIR OWN NAMES

1. Parent writes child's name in script, using thick felt pen. Parent indicates sequence and direction of strokes.
   Child *writes over* the letters of the name.
   Initially, parent may guide child's hand.
2. Parent writes child's name in script; indicates sequence of strokes.
   Child traces name using tracing, or similar, paper.
3. Parent writes child's name in script.
   Child copies own name.

This over-writing, tracing and copying sequence teaches writing and spelling together. The most important word in the world, so far as the child is concerned, can be read and understood. Once children can copy their names, they feel that they have made their marks. We cannot emphasize too strongly, however, that if the child is to be really helped, then, from the start, each letter must be started correctly and made by the correct sequence of strokes. Unless this is carefully and scrupulously monitored and controlled children can produce perfect copies which, in fact, have been written backwards from right to left!

In Appendices 1 and 2, we give details of the sequence of strokes and suggestions for facilitating the construction of all letters. Sticking to this procedure will obviate the possibility that children will have a lot of unlearning to do later, or that their writing disintegrates when they are put under pressure to write notes when they are 10 years old and over. Moreover, things learned correctly in infancy and the early years stay with us and will never be so easy to learn when we are older.

The children will want to keep a copy of their names from which to copy when they have finished a painting or drawing. As their drawings may contain members of the immediate family and family pets, their names will have to be learned in similar fashion. Later, too, the children will want to write their full names, their addresses (often ending up with The Milky Way, The Universe!), and their ages.

The next step is usually when children want to put titles on their pictures. Parents will know that nothing is more devastating for children than to be asked, 'What's that?' As the pictures are what they say they are, we must ask them to tell us about their pictures. Then we can suggest the appropriate title, such as, 'Daddy and the baby' or 'My swing'. Negotiating the right title is important. We want the children to know exactly what they have decided. Their first response may have been, 'It's me with my ball and there's daddy and that there is . . .' Again, we will begin by writing in thick felt pen for over-writing, go on to tracing and only finally expect the children to copy. But, however they may have written the titles, we will want them to read them to us. Because they know the title, they will be able to read what they wrote.

As children's pictures are executed quickly and frequently, it is possible to introduce them to a wide vocabulary and to the writing and spelling of a lot of words. In the process, they will be learning the letter shapes, their names and sounds, as well as the common sequences of letters and words. All this helps reading, too.

Many parents, during this early stage of learning to write and spell, make cards for labelling places and things around the house. 'Pat's toy cupboard', 'Tristram's room', 'Scruff's basket' etc. may well have to adorn the house for a few weeks. Use upper and lower case and only very exceptionally write words in capital letters only. Try to keep the letters grouped together, not spread out unnaturally. Attention to these details, and to the regular shape of the letters, will improve their recognition.

Special Secret Words

When Sylvia Ashton Warner taught Maori children, she found one way of really getting them interested in writing and reading was to ask them to think of their own special word, one they thought was the best word they knew. When the children had chosen their own words and whispered them to her, she wrote them out on cards and each child was given his or her own special word. 'Kiss' and 'ghost' were popular words! The children had no difficulty in remembering and recognizing their own word, of course. Parents can adopt a similar approach. The Special Secret Word can be over-written, traced and copied. It can become the first in a collection of word cards which, together with all the other word cards for labels and picture titles, can be kept in alphabetical order in an old box and used as the First Dictionary or Wordstore, itself suitably labelled. These words, with their different lengths and shapes, with their various patterns of letters, all of which have been written and traced and copied, teach the children what goes on on the surface of reading. It is under this surface that the meaning lies. Now they are learning to read by writing, by encoding their own language in print. It is here that the subskills of reading, the sounds and sequences of letters, are best learned.

When a dozen or so cards have been made, traced and copied, they can be used for games such as First Letter Snap or Last Letter Snap. These games, with their turn-taking and element of surprise, are simple to devise to meet children's interests and needs, and prepare the way for more sophisticated games. But enthusiastic parents with a little time to spare can manufacture word cards and quickly build up a powerful wordstore with enormous potential.

Home, Sweet Printing House

By making a profusion of cards for common and special words used by our children, home can become a veritable printing house. There are some simple principles, however, which it is useful to observe.

HOW TO BUILD A WORDSTORE

* Start with words known and used by the children.
* Introduce new words in this order:
    1. Word labelling real thing or picture.
    2. Word labelling diagram.
    3. Word only.
* At each of the three stages the children over-write, trace and copy the word, saying the word as they write it and naming each letter.
* At each stage play a matching game in which the children's copy of the word is matched with the card mixed in with other cards.
* Place the word-only card in the wordstore.
* From time to time, go through the wordstore in random order with the children naming each card immediately it appears.

The reason for this sequence is to make sure that the children go from the concrete thing or its realistic picture, then to a sign or diagram of the thing before being expected to remember the abstract symbol, the word, for the thing. We can appreciate the importance of this if we reflect on our own experience of becoming familiar with a new piece of equipment in the home. First, we 'play' with it, we study the controls and the symbols on them. We may then look at the diagrams in the manual to find out more about the various functions. Then we will read the manual. Rarely do we read the manual or instructions before familiarizing ourselves with the equipment; rarely do we read the text without reference to the diagrams. Our children need the same familiarity with words before we should expect them to deal with the abstract symbols of print. This method takes care of that, whilst providing three opportunities for the children to learn to write each word.

The little words or function words cannot all be represented either pictorially or diagrammatically. However, these words appear so frequently that they will be learned in use during the next stage of the wordstore's use. Some function words can be illustrated, of course, and this may well help in the early days of setting up the store.

and	to	from	by	over	under	in
+	→	←	→|	•̄	⎯•	⊔↓

The biggest problem parents find is of having enough of each of
them when the wordstore is operational.

Wordstore to Word Processor

Starting from playing the game of **Find the card that says . . .**, it is
a natural progression to suggest, **What can we say with these
cards?**, whilst displaying on the table or floor cards, say, for 'milk'
and 'glass' or 'milk' and 'cat'. When the children suggest 'a glass of
milk' or 'the cat is drinking the milk', the extra words needed can be
drawn by them from the wordstore and laid out in sequence. If
words are not in the store they can quickly be printed and added to it
after the children have learned to write them. Generating sentences
in this way, encouraging the children to make sentences and then
stories with the words in the wordstore, demonstrates what is involved in encoding language in print and is particularly enjoyed by
children because it produces rapid results. They quickly become
adept at finding the right word cards and arranging them in line in
the correct sequence. Mistakes can be quickly corrected and sentences can be readily changed to alter their meanings. It is recommended that work with the word processor is begun *before* the
wordstore is loaded with all the words in all their forms (plurals,
present, past and future tenses of verbs and all the auxiliaries). This
is because it is rare that we can anticipate all the words we would
need and it is far better to provide them as and when they are
needed. In this way, the children learn that, usually, an 's' has to be
added for plurals, that some words, verbs, change according to
number and time, and that the little words cannot be ignored or the
meaning will not be plain.

If some pieces of card and a felt pen are kept handy, it is far better
to supply the word cards, therefore, 'on demand' and the children
will enjoy discovering new words to add to the wordstore.

When the children are sufficiently advanced with their own writing and spelling, in connection, for example, with the activities
described later in this chapter, the wordstore may not only be used
as a dictionary to help them spell the words they need, it may also be

used to plan their own stories. Now the children select the words they need, arrange them in order, and then copy them out. They will be helped in this if they are encouraged to plan a sentence at a time. This planning shows the children the importance of thinking about what they are going to say, of marshalling the words they need in advance, of thinking in sentences and of having the patterns of print and of writing 'at their finger tips'. Planning in this way will also help them to see, in advance, if there are any new words they will need to ask us how to spell before starting to write. Once more we are building bridges and providing help and support for our children without exposing them to unnecessary difficulties and to failure. But, above all, the wordstore and word processor approach to writing and to reading is a hands-on, participatory, interactive way of learning about how language works.

When, some years ago, teachers used a similar approach to this in the Breakthrough to Literacy Project of the Schools Council, many realized how much better it was to use their own word cards and wordstore, built up with the children, rather than the carefully prepared and well presented ready-mades. And there was one great advantage discerning teachers discovered. The children soon found out that they needed a special vocabulary to talk about the kinds of words they needed. Instead of just looking for the word in the store, they were looking for 'an *s* to make it plural', asking for 'another word to say what sort of dress she's wearing', demanding a word 'that says what he's doing'. Parents can be on the look out for this development in language consciousness. They need not fear if, later on, they are using words like noun, verb, adverb and adjective, that they are being old-fashioned or out of step with syntax and linguistics. If they are using words to order and classify in this way, not even the philosopher Wittgenstein would have disputed their good sense in doing so! Teachers who, in the past (for we cannot imagine there are any surviving), believed that grammar was unnecessary and even stood in the way of children's 'creativity', were denying the children access to language itself. To talk about language without using grammatical terms is as fatuous as trying to talk about mathematics without using its language of terms for functions, computation and shapes such as prime, fraction, multiply, circle and logarithm. *Using language with our children means using it to amplify their thinking. The more power tools of thought we can give them the better.*

If our children's written expression of their thoughts is to be unimpeded, however, they need an efficient writing system. So far we have only discussed this in connection with starting them off writing their own names. As valuable as this incidental teaching is, it is essential that writing and spelling are taught parallel to their development of reading and word-processing skills.

Letter Shapes in Print

Getting the right letter shapes made in the right sequence of strokes is the foundation of efficient handwriting. Perfectly shaped letters made the wrong way round will prove inefficient and, once speed is demanded in, for instance, note-taking, the shapes will disintegrate too. In Appendix 1, the correct sequence of strokes for each letter is shown. Appendix 5 gives the order in which the letters may be taught most efficiently and exercised in the writing of words and common letter strings. Parents are much better placed than teachers for making sure that children adopt the right posture and maintain it during writing. Although parents may be busy about the home attending to many things while they are keeping an eye on what their children are doing, they rarely have twenty or thirty children competing for their time and attention. The big advantage we have as parents is that we can usually give close and intense help when our children need it with the tasks in which they are involved. With learning to write this is vitally important.

THREE POINTS TO WATCH WITH WRITING

1. Right posture.
2. Relaxed pencil hold.
3. Right sequence of strokes in the right direction.

During these early years we can expect that many children will read and write lying prone on the floor or rolled up in a ball under a table. We also have to admit that it is not uncommon to find that children who appear to be doing the neatest and best handwriting, often adopt the most unconventional postures and grips. However, as with playing a musical instrument or performing any skill, the earlier a correct posture is adopted, the easier development and mastery will be. Children will have had opportunity to experiment with different hands and different grips with brushes, crayons and pencils. Now we need to establish efficient gross and fine motor skills. Handedness, which starts being established from about the first birthday, will usually be evident by 3 years of age. The majority of children, 90 per cent in the UK, being right-handed, are readily identified. Ambidextrous children cause little concern and will be helped if the right hand is established as the preferred hand for writing. Left-handed children may reveal their preferred hand in feeding themselves, but often it is not until they start to write that they need special help or even show a strong preference for their left hand. We set out below the postures suitable for right- and left-handed children respectively.

WRITING POSTURE — RIGHT-HANDED WRITERS

* Seated, both feet firmly on floor, left leading slightly.
* Trunk upright and leaning slightly forward.
* Right forearm resting on table.
* Left hand steadying paper with hand open, palm down, index finger and thumb on left edge of paper or book.
* Paper placed to the right of writer, tilted downward to the left.
* Check that child has unobstructed view of paper.
* Check that the right wrist rests lightly on paper and can move smoothly to right across paper.

The posture for the left-handed writers ensures that they have a clear view of what they have written. Some experimentation may be necessary in the early days until the children decide, from experience of writing, which of the alternative positions of the hand they prefer.

WRITING POSTURE — LEFT-HANDED WRITERS

* Seated, both feet firmly on floor, right leading slightly.
* Trunk upright and leaning slightly forward.
* Left forearm resting on table.
* Right hand steadying paper with hand open, palm down, index finger and thumb on right edge of paper or book.

* Paper placed to the left of the writer but tilted downward to the right.
* Left wrist resting lightly on paper *below* writing line,

OR

Left wrist turned at right angles, side of hand resting lightly on paper *above* the writing line.

Initially, the children will tend to grip the pencil or ballpoint pen tightly, the whites of their knuckles showing just how firmly they are gripping and concentrating on what they are doing. A relaxed hold should be encouraged.

RELAXED WRITING HOLD

* The pencil should be resting on the second finger against which it is lightly held by the thumb and index finger.
* The first joint of the index finger should not be pressed or bent in.
* Check that, if the pencil is gently tugged, it slides out from between fingers and thumb.
* Relaxation will come with confidence and encouragement to relax, rather than demands not to grip.

In the home it is not easy to have a variety of desks and chairs tailor-made to meet the requirements of ever-growing children. It helps if the children can sit on a cushion, or pile of newspapers, on top of the ordinary sized adult chair and have a stool or box on which to rest their feet, if the dining or kitchen table is used. When they first start writing, we can help the children to adopt the correct posture and begin to write correctly if we stand behind them and take their hands in ours to guide their fingers through the sequence of strokes. This will help them to get the feel of writing much more quickly than explanations. Again, praise for what they have got right is better than reading the riot act for what they have got wrong. If they could get it right, they wouldn't have anything to learn!

The act of writing, if the children can see what they are writing while they are writing it, provides visual and tactile feedback of what is being done. This means that the pattern of strokes and their sequence is being doubly reinforced. If they are being performed correctly, they will be well learned. If performed incorrectly, there will be a lot of unlearning to do. When children start learning to write they need a lot of short, intense practice sessions with careful supervision to make sure that they are learning to write correctly.

GETTING WRITING RIGHT

* Make sure children know the letter, its shape and sound.
* Demonstrate the starting point for making the letter.
* Show the direction from the starting point.
* Show the sequence of strokes.
* Provide a diagram showing the above.
* Teach the child what to say when writing: for example, 'Pee says puh for poppy: down the stem, up and round for the poppy'
* Use lined paper to assist both with a level writing line and with the proportion of the parts of letters.
* Start each line with written examples for over-writing.
* Finish each line with examples for over-writing; this ensures that the children finish the line making as perfect a letter as possible.

Anyone who has ever had to write 'lines' knows that if a task is repeated over and over again, without thought, then there is a strong possibility that the writing will deteriorate. Finishing each line with over-writing will help to prevent this happening, but the biggest contribution will be made by the parents' praise for what is right. If the children also say the name and the sound of the letter and talk themselves through the sequence of strokes they will soon get the shape automatized and coming off the ends of their fingers. Their fingers will be imprinted with the pattern of print.

When children first start to write, plain paper is essential, as they have so little control of the pencil and so little idea of letter shapes and their orientation. When they start learning to write and spell, lined paper will help them. By using three lines of narrow lined paper they are given clear guidance concerning the height of the ascenders, the size of the bodies and the depth of the descenders. When they go on to the next lines of writing there is no danger of tops and tails getting mixed up with one another. This keeps a clear, uncluttered view of what has already been written. Parents who look at each line as it is completed and comment favourably on their children's progress can also suggest points which still need attention. By saying, for example, 'Those *o*s are just the right size. That's great – keep them like that and try to close them at the top so that they keep the rain out!' we can help them to get things right. In learning skills we must prevent them from practising errors! If the scheme outlined in Appendix 5 is followed, then the children will be learning to write and spell simultaneously. However, we will help them best if we encourage them to gradually change from subvocalizing the letter names, sounds and strokes to saying to themselves the sounds of the syllables or letter strings as they write them. Then, once the syllables and strings have been automatized this can be faded out. We once thought that subvocalization should be discouraged in both reading to oneself and in writing. Research has shown, however, that no matter how fast one reads, neural activity can be detected in the speech areas of the throat. As there are such obvious advantages in encouraging children to talk themselves through these essential but complex little skills, we now encourage them to do so until they no longer need to.

SEQUENCE OF 'TALKING THROUGH' WRITING AND SPELLING

1. When learning letters: say name, sound and sequence of strokes.
2. When learning words: say word and sounds of syllables and letter strings.
3. When writing sentences: say words.

Writing Patterns to Spelling

Our spelling system is part historical and part convention and the best attitude we can have towards it is that, like Mount Everest, we must conquer it because it is there. It is nice to invent excuses for its inconsistencies but what we have to accept is that there is no connection at all between sound and sense, or between spelling and sound or sense. The sound of *no* is the same as the sound of *know* and, although the redundant *k* may owe its existence to the Latin, Greek and Sanskrit roots of *know*, that doesn't account for the fact that we spell *nous* and *noology*, the science of intellect, without it! Even the spelling rules we learned are best remembered as warnings that they don't work when we need them! 'I before E except after C' doesn't work with *seize*, and doubling the final consonant after a vowel before adding *-ed* or *-ing* doesn't apply to words of more than two syllables such as *benefited*. How then do we manage to spell so well – or put another way, why were newspapers better spelt before the advances of high tech? The answer is that we have *visual* memories of the shape and spelling of words we have seen thousands of times and *kinaesthetic* or physical memories of words we have written thousands of times. That is why, when asked how to spell difficult words, we like to scribble them down, look at what we've written and decide if they look right. We use the word 'scribble' deliberately because we want our fingers to write the word rather than have our intellect get in the way and start dictating. Of course, this only works with words we are familiar with. Dyslexic children, who haven't been reading for six years, are going to need years of reading experience, after they have learned to read, before they can hope to catch up with their spelling – unless someone has the sense to teach them how to automatize spelling through their fingers in just the same way that many of them have already been taught to play musical instruments.

Spelling and handwriting must be learned not spurned, and taught not caught. That is certainly true for the majority of children and, even for the tiny minority who do seem to have been pre-wired with the skills, practice makes perfect. As with speech, of course, elegant and efficient examples help, too. Parents whose own handwriting is poor and unformed will find that demonstrating letter shapes using full arm, rather than finger, movements will produce better shapes. It is only a matter of making the effort. We can all learn to write with our other hand or our feet if necessary. There are some excellent books on the market by calligraphers, but don't try introducing young pre-school children to italic styles based on the lozenge or diamond shape, as this is beyond their abilities. Once the basic print shapes are written fluently, children can start joined up, or double writing, as they call the cursive style. In view of what we have said already, there is an obvious advantage in having an efficient and simple method of joining letters together. It is this act of joining letters that go together to make sounds and words that helps us to spell them together. It is these patterns we remember and which, in reading, help us to predict what comes next.

Patterns that Predict

In fact, our spelling is much more consistent than many people believe. It is the regularity and consistency we need to emphasize when teaching young children. This is particularly important because children are programmed to notice differences. Teach what is regular and the children will see the irregularities. Give them the patterns and they will see the exceptions. In Appendix 5, we list some of the common patterns and clusters in the common words in which they are used. By writing the words in sentences, they will make the links of spelling and sound to that which unites them, the meaning of language. Similarly, by using words which go together or are linked by some common feature, they will associate them in families. For example,

We can see the green beech trees.

That sentence not only exercises writing the *ee* but links it to common words like *see* and *green* whilst establishing that the *beech* (happily, for it is no more than a coincidence) uses the *ee* which appears in *tree*. This aid to memorization needs to be separated, until it is well established, from similar aids, with which we do not want it to be confused. For example,

The seal lay on the beach out of reach of the sea.

The same method can be used later when children encounter words they find difficult to spell. A notoriously difficult word for children is *scissors* (sissers, sisers, cicers, sissors, etc.) which will be a little easier to remember, perhaps, if written out in this sentence:

For science at school tomorrow we need scissors and mirrors or Sir will scent blood.

But such aids can only be deployed to help our children if they have been given every help from the start to write and spell simple words and frequently recurring words quickly and clearly.

Words that Sound what They Mean

One way of helping children get to grips with the sounds of speech and the letters we use to represent them is to give them some Goon Show fun with imitative and onomatopoeic words, such as Crunch, Bang, Zigzag, Pop, Splatter and Zoom. We list them in all their banal glory in Appendix 4. With them we can play games such as 'What goes . . .?' and 'What noise does a . . . make?' The more zany nonsense that can be introduced into this, the more language-conscious we will make our children. And, in the realm of language and its uses and abuses, a sense of the ridiculous is essential.

If these onomatopoeic words are used to introduce the spelling and writing of the sounds they represent, many children will be helped to grasp the encoding system. Unfortunately, unlike Chinese, we cannot demonstrate any connection between the appearance of words in their alphabetic spelling and their meaning. But we can cheat!

Look! Making Words Look Like what They Mean

Poets, deprived of ideograms, pictograms and icons, have written religious poems in the shape of crosses and stars and love poems in the shape of hearts and flowers. Guillaume Apollinaire called his visual poetry calligrams. More recently, there has been a vogue of concrete poetry. Calligrams are to the eye what onomatopoeic words are to the ear. We mention these deep cultural roots because we would not like parents to think that they are being diverted into activities which have anything but the most respectable academic antecedents! Our serious purpose, of course, is that the children and their parents have fun. Calligrams help to bring print alive and help us to see it in what William James called its 'sensational nudity'. For children who find the 'damned squiggly black marks' forbidding, calligrams cut print down to size and turn it into a thing we can play around with. For everyone, calligrams make us look at how words are made and remember them and how they are spelled.

PU??LED   PUDown   DR P o

sPLash

L c o m o tivE

SCissors / SCissors

MIRROR

Once children have seen us make a few calligrams, they are keen to make their own. If they can help them remember words with which they have difficulty, whether in reading or spelling, so much the better. They are particularly useful in helping children to remember words with double consonants in them, such as *middle* and *little*, and in helping them to get used to building up longer words, such as *earthquake* and *waterfall*. Fortunately, once we introduce children to this form of play with words, as with puns, for these *are* visual puns, they will discover that opportunities to use them abound. Children who are developing an interest in drawing will find calligrams give them new ways of developing their skill. For those children who still find it difficult to express themselves graphically, we can help them by showing them how to use stencils, Letraset or something similar, or, easiest of all, letters cut out from magazines and pasted in position.

WAYS WITH CALLIGRAMS

* Freehand with ballpoint, fibretips of various thickness and colour.
* Cut-out letters stuck where we want them.
* Stencils, Letraset or similar, or by drawing round letter shapes.

* Combining pictures of things and their printed names in collages.
* Animating words with micro graphics.

The progression from calligraphic words to verse is a useful step, especially when we wish to encourage our children to use their newly acquired writing skills to make up and write sentences.

From Calligrams to Concrete Verse

Here the aim is to make what we say look like what we are writing about, in exactly the same way as, it will be remembered, Lewis Carroll did with the Mouse's Tale, which runs punningly down the page like a mouse's tail. It is amazing that of the millions of children who have enjoyed the Mouse's Tale, so few have been encouraged to try making something like it themselves. Yet, whenever we have suggested to children that they might like to see what they could do, the response has always been enthusiastic.

The approach which we have found works best is to get the children thinking and talking about something we know they find exciting. What would they like to see at a circus? Which animals would they like to see in the wild? What's the best firework display/Christmas tree/bonfire/storm/ or most beautiful scene they have ever seen? What's the most frightening/horrible/ghastly/ghostly thing they've heard in a story? Then, whether they tell us that, 'The great big lion jumped through the flaming ring', or that 'They trembled with fear as the thunder boomed and the lightning flashed', we can write their key sentence out for them and discuss how it can be written to look like the event. There are many ways in which this may be done. We can repeat the words over and over again so that they make the shape of the event or the subject; or the words may be arranged so that they depict some aspect of the subject. Using colour, of course, greatly increases the opportunities of making a picture with words but often the most telling effects are produced by the simplest means. What matters is that our children exercise their imaginations, their language and their spelling and writing skills.

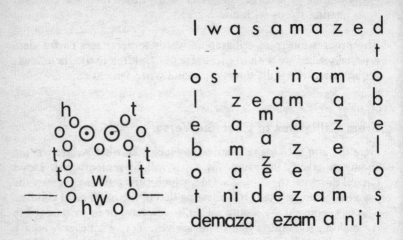

So far, we have been discussing developing writing and spelling skills, not in isolation, but in the context of language. There is no denying, however, that the skills have to be developed and exercised with care and attention, and that the various suggestions we have made are essentially opportunities for making the process as enjoyable and as purposeful as possible for both parents and children. Parallel with the development of write-and-spell, children need the opportunity to express themselves in writing. This is provided by the Language Experience approach better than by any other of which we are aware.

The Language Experience Approach

This approach to reading through writing is the most logical imaginable. It has been used in schools in the USA where, after a false start, it has become well established, in Canada, Australasia and Britain. It begins when we ask children to tell us about their pictures, write down what they say and get them to over-write, trace and copy it. When they show us what they have written we ask them to read what it says, and they *can* read what it says because they knew what it meant when they wrote it! If we think of the problem confronting a child who can already read a little and has to make sense of such simple words as, 'I think, so I am' or 'To be or not to be', or wishes to read a simple tale and is immediately confronted with names like Rumpelstiltskin or Thumbelina, we can appreciate how much easier and safer it is to start out reading what one knows.

The reason why the Language Experience approach is not used more extensively in schools is quite understandable. It is demanding of time and individual attention is essential. Many teachers use Language Experience in the earliest stages, especially with titles to children's pictures, but it is less common to find LE being used to its full potential and developed into Language Exchange and Language Networking as we describe them here. But teachers with good rapport with young children and excellent class management skills have found that LE soon gets children writing and reading on their own and develops these skills on the best of sound foundations, the children's own thoughts and language.

The very disadvantages for harassed teachers in crowded classrooms are the very advantages of the approach for parents. LE is individual and arises out of the children's experience and the language they use to describe it. It puts children in the hands-on position of the first people to record their own words or thoughts at the very beginning of the encoding process. The only difference is that our children inherit an alphabetic system of twenty-six letters in which to record the forty-four sound units of English. With this they are already familiar, partly from their shared and paired reading experience and partly from word cards and from write-and-spell.

Listing to Literacy by LE

Some years ago, we investigated how people used written language in their everyday lives, in order to determine how best to help children develop written language in as natural and as functional a way as possible. We found that, contrary to our expectations, letter writing was by no means the chief use to which we put writing. At the top of the list came list making itself. At the bottom of the list, even amongst academics and professional writers, came essay writing, that most difficult of forms which is so oddly beloved of schools and colleges cocooned from the usages of life. List making was closely followed by note making, a form of jotting down which is very much akin to list making. Messages and reports, including accounts of events and simple narratives, came next. It is this order of priorities we have found most closely meets the needs of parents and children in finding opportunities for Language Experience at home.

For children who have been writing word cards and picture titles, the obvious place to start LE is list making. One jumping-off place is the shopping list, which helps children to feel really useful and important and doing something for real. If a board or jotter pad is kept in the kitchen and used for jotting down items, this can be used as the starting point. No matter how we begin, it is essential that the children talk through the items with us first and that they are familiar with the items being listed. When the final list has been drawn up, the children copy it out. It is at this stage that items with which they are unfamiliar can be left out. When the shopping has been brought home they check out the items they have listed, calling out the items and crossing them off their list. Of course, if they have been on the shopping trip they will have had opportunity to use their list then, too. Used in this way, the shopping list quickly familiarizes children with many common words, which will also be seen by them on packets, wrappings and in advertisements. It also helps them to understand that it is not always necessary to write everything down: one word may stand for many. For instance, 'Vegetables' might be on the list to indicate 'Buy what vegetables are available in the shop/ market today'; 'Tea, 2' may stand for 'two packets of Twiddlers' Green Label'. Other items, however, may be written in full in order to be sure we get precisely what we want and do not forget a small but significant detail. Opportunities for writing lists, apart from shopping, will soon come to mind with children who are involved in the daily life of the home. Here are some examples:

LIST MAKING FOR EARLY LANGUAGE EXPERIENCE WRITING

* Menus   'What will we have for . . .?'
* Recipes   'How do we make . . .?' 'What do we need for . . .?'
* Toy cupboard   'What toys are in this box/cupboard?'
  contents
* Book lists   'What books have we?' 'What books have I read/
                   borrowed?'

* Itineraries   'Where have we been?' 'Where are we going?'
* Inventories   'What shall we need for the beach/park/picnic, etc.?'
* Family tree   'Who is in our family?'
* Favourites   Pets, People, Clothes, Colours, Meat, Vegetables, Fruit, Drink, Flowers, Trees, etc.
* Messages   'Remember to tell Mum/Dad/whoever that . . .'
                      'When we write to . . . we must tell them about . . .'
                      'Ring the garage/doctor's surgery about . . .'

It is not suggested that all or any of these opportunities should be taken unless they interest the parents and their children, and unless they can be briefly talked about and quickly written and copied out. There may well be many other opportunities which are far more significant and these should be used. Family birthdays and high days and holidays, which mean so much to children, may well give opportunities for them to talk about sending notes to family and friends which can then be written out for them and carefully copied. What makes this a Language Experience piece of writing is that, *once written by the child it is then read*. LE is thinking about experience, talking about experience, writing down what was said and reading back what was written. It is this sequence which separates LE from the common chore, valuable though it may be, of simply putting one's name on a printed birthday card.

Developing LE

Once LE has been introduced, it can be developed along two lines:

* *Diary or News* – 'What have we done today?'
* *Stories* – 'Tell the story of . . .' (Retelling of a known tale.)
         'Make up a story about . . .'

In both instances, the child talks first and only writes down what has been said. In both instances, in the early stages, the parent will write down the child's words for the child to copy.

Gradually, as the child becomes more able in all the skills, parental preparation will be phased out. *But the LE cycle will not have been completed until the children 'read what they wrote and know what it means, because they knew what they meant when they wrote it'.* It may well be that parents will order the children's string of words into simple sentences and make some minor alterations in the choice and variety of words, but these changes will be made clear as the parents write out the story for the child to copy. It is not intended that children should tell the stories in their entirety. Three or four sentences at a time will be more than enough and stories may well be spread over a number of days. This will give opportunities for re-reading.

It is strongly urged that children are encouraged to begin each sentence on a new line in these early stages. The ritual of beginning each sentence with a capital letter and of ending with a full stop will be more quickly learned if the 'new sentence, new line' policy is adopted. This policy should be continued into the next stage in which children make up and write their own stories unaided. It will help them to avoid the common 'And then' syndrome of stringing stories together.

Parents and teachers who see their children absorbed in their favourite TV programmes are sometimes tempted to ask them to write about them. This is usually a disappointing experience and one best left until the children are experienced story tellers and over 10 years of age. It is much easier to get children to write about their own first-hand experience, both in the news and diary form, or as a story. They can be encouraged to do this if we suggest to them an incident in their recent experience or if we remind them of a story they enjoy hearing about themselves 'when they were little'. Again, we get them to talk through the event first. Here are some subjects we have found which are likely to start children off when they ask 'What shall I write about?' (and we are invariably busy and thinking of something else!) or when we want to stimulate them to tell us a tale.

TALES FOR CHILDREN TO TELL FOR LE

* When I was little.
* When I was naughty. When someone else was naughty.
* When I was brave.
* Tales about living, lively things like themselves – puppies, cubs, ducklings, lambs, calves.
* About getting lost, and found.

* About finding something/someone, but usually treasure.
* About magic – wizards, magic stones, wishes.
* About secret caves.
* About how animals got their spots/feathers/teeth/tusks, etc.
* About ghosts in castles.
* About wicked pirates or smugglers.
* About changing into something else – metamorphosis.

If you want to save yourself time, write key words for the above ingredients on separate cards, then, when you want a story, shuffle the cards, deal yourself three or four and you will have mixed yourself a tale! Maybe your child's LE story will become another classic. What is remarkable about Daisy Ashford's *The Young Visiters* is not that it is a delightful story written by 9-year-old Daisy in 1890, but that it was published. With the opportunities that the LE programme provides for the continuous development of written language, many children can be helped to write equally entertaining stories.

Developing Children's Skills

When children have enjoyed these experiences of writing their news and stories and of reading them back, they can progress to retelling stories they have enjoyed or to writing their own stories, without first telling them to their parents and having them written out. They will be helped in this if they can use the word card store which has been built up, or can use a simple picture dictionary. A careful check should still be kept on their handwriting and spelling. One way of doing this, without damming the flow of their imaginations, is to encourage them to regard their first attempt as a draft which, with help, will be revised, improved and corrected. Here, we should try to get them to look for the sentences which may be improved and for the errors which they can correct. This is just what authors and journalists do. It is only in schools that the process of correction is regarded as ignominious. Once corrected, then, with great pride, they can make their own fair copy. It is this which they will then read aloud.

When children are writing their own stories for LE, it is often

131

helpful to them if they are encouraged to shut their eyes, think about what they want to say and only then write it down. We have found that doing this helps many children to organize their thoughts, to find the words they need and to use their imaginations to greater effect. Why this should be so, and why it should so often result in children writing in language so rich in imagery that it is sometimes difficult to believe that they wrote it, we do not know. Wordsworth perhaps provides a clue, when he writes of poetry being emotion recollected in tranquillity.

Networking – LE Exchange

The progress children make in writing and reading through the LE approach is quite considerable. Schools found that children not only enjoyed listening to one another read their stories, they wanted to *read* one another's stories. In some areas, this resulted in exchanging stories between children in the same class, then between classes in the same school and finally between schools. Nothing, of course, could be greater proof of the benefits of the LE approach. Just as the proof of the value of paired reading is when children read, on their own, books they have never seen before, so the proof of the LE pudding is when children read other children's stories. They have gone from knowing what the writing means because they wrote it, to reading what other people wrote and knowing what they meant.

Children find great appeal in what other children have written. The closeness of experience, interests and language accounts, in part, for this but, in our experience, it is often the little differences to which young children are sensitive. They are rarely critical of one another's work and are, instead, accepting and eager to enjoy and applaud. Parents who have started their children on LE find that it is remarkably easy to arrange exchanges within the family, between neighbours and friends and through contacts with other parents, of children of similar age to their own, at work or at nursery and play schools. Children who have successfully swopped their stories between brothers and sisters and their friends will need little encouragement to spread the network wider.

Networking in this way needs parental monitoring to avoid difficulties with stories that may present problems of legibility and comprehensibility. As the stories are likely to be short, it is a simple matter to use the paired-reading technique with them to avoid disappointment. But difficulties such as these bring out into the open the importance of legibility and correct spelling. They are not empty conventions but vital components of communication, as important as clear and comprehensible speech. Parents have found that networking also helps them to see problems in perspective, to accept differences in reading and writing development as in physical development, and to share information, ideas and experience. When parents find that exchanging their children's stories is proving mutually advantageous, they may well go on to exchange books and, thereby, discover new authors and subjects to keep their children book-hooked.

The essence of networking is that it is cooperative mutual aid. If it grows organically, serving the happiness and success of the children in a mutually supportive and cooperative way, it is fine. But, if networking gets contaminated by competitiveness and the odour of comparisons, it should be abandoned.

Forms of LE Writing

When children start writing their stories and begin reading and hearing tongue-twisters, riddles, jokes, poetry and verse, they often develop very much like the young Dylan Thomas. He confessed that, when he started to write, he would have tried his little trotters at anything! News and stories are but starting points. Children will write poetry and verse, given a little encouragement, as happily as a shopping list. They will write what Dylan Thomas called the 'tumble and rhyme' of everyday speech and revel in it. Some will write with telling simplicity of the most deeply felt emotions or of the most profound insights, so that we are reminded of William Blake or Stevie Smith. We are not suggesting here that children are 'natural' writers. We are saying categorically that young children, uninhibited by failure and other people's standards and criticisms, will adventure with words and make what they can with them. If we encourage them, and feed them with richness and variety, they will write jingles, pop songs, nonsense verse, limericks, skipping rhymes, parodies, couplets, make logos and slogans, ballads, clerihews, haiku, tongue-twisters, cartoon strip stories, calypsos and sonnets. This was the variety of children's writing shown to us by children in a working-class area as examples of the writing they did at home. Some children produced books of their own work. All were no more than 10 years of age. Schools which have stimulated such richness have found, as Connie and Harold Rosen wrote in their report for the Schools Council, *The Language of Primary School Children* (1973):

> Now we can see it [children's writing] as the development of a new medium of expression with its own unique possibilities for enabling children to understand and act in their world.

The stimulation of home throughout the pre-school and early years of schooling, is uniquely placed to foster children's writing. Parental encouragement to experiment and parental praise for achievement, no matter how modest, will help our children to grow up better able to express themselves and better able to understand and to appreciate what others have written. It is essential that we develop this sensitivity to the diverse uses of language in children who will grow up into a world in which information will flood into our homes and work places. Only if they have values, standards, knowledge and wisdom will they be able to evaluate it and process it. If we have encouraged them to write, we will have begun by giving them Language Experience which is the beginning of awareness and understanding.

The Achievement of LE and Paired Reading

The child who has learned to read by paired reading can say, 'The first book I read and enjoyed, I read with my parents'. The child who has learned to read by LE can say, 'The first book I read and enjoyed, when I read it on my own, was the first book I wrote myself'. Children who have begun to read in these ways have been given a foundation in the encoding and decoding of language which is at the heart of the reading process. They have taken a giant step forward into literacy which will stand them in good stead for the rest of their lives. John Dewey summed it up when he wrote: 'Children are people. They grow into tomorrow only as they live today.'

8

Making the Programme Work

So far, we have concentrated on describing the sequences of development from lap learning to paired reading and Language Experience as if everyone was starting to prepare in pregnancy. Of course, many parents will want to start when they have read this book and when, in fact, their children have already advanced some steps along the way. For all parents, no matter when, where or how they start, there are certain general principles which apply equally, but which have to be interpreted differently according to each child's circumstances, needs and abilities. Some are self-evident but we include them to avoid any possible misunderstanding.

STARTING SUCCESSFULLY

* Always start at a point at which the child is fully able to understand, fully able to respond and fully able to achieve success.
* Always go back to a point at which the child is absolutely confident and secure.
* Starting with guaranteed success and confidence, give tasks or ask questions which enable the child to show what is known or to demonstrate ability, and immediately reward achievement with praise.
* Build success upon success, especially initially, by advancing on a gentle gradient of difficulty.
* The natural style for parental teaching is incidental interaction taken 'on the wing'. Use a light touch, teach incidentally or in a game-playing situation if possible.
* Teach when the child is eager and alert and keen to cooperate.
* Stimulate interest, simulate your own enthusiasm if the task is not particularly appealing at the time, go for maximum involvement, intense concentration and finish fast before interest wanders.
* Finish on high achievement and the reward of success.

* Be guided by the child's interest and enthusiasm.
* In cases of apparent inexplicable difficulties, ask the child, who may be able to tell you.

If one remembers how quickly conversational exchanges take place with out children in the early years and observes how long they concentrate on one activity when playing, it is soon apparent that most children will often only apply themselves with complete absorption for a few minutes. Even when we read to them and they are thoroughly absorbed in a favourite story, they may soon begin to fidget or to fall asleep. So, whether we are starting with shared or paired reading, or a painting for an LE title, a little and often is better than a lot of rot! Even when children themselves appear keen to continue, if attention appears to be fading or quality of response is declining, finish on a high and promise more on an early occasion. On no account think that, because progress is being made, doubling the dose will double the attainment. Never exceed the sated dose!

A Natural Parental Style

Parents are individuals and we are entitled to respect for our own needs and individuality. Although we have indicated the need for clear speech and dramatic reading, for a lively manner and a sense of fun, we recognize that parents will interpret these differently. What is important is to find a natural and relaxed style into which one can slip which is congenial to both oneself and one's child. That is far more important than forced brightness or attempting to don the bustling manner of some best forgotten teacher. Sometimes it is hard to get enthusiastic about a Eustace Bear or Naughty Gnu and we may well have to act as if we shared our child's fascination and delight. But we should avoid acting Teacher. We have known delectable and gentle ladies transformed into shrill shrews and cool, laid-back men of the world transmogrified into dervish drill sergeants when they acted a traditional teacher. It is an interesting fact that the stereotype of a teacher in cartoons and comics is a Dracula-like figure in mortarboard and gown, wielding a stick and on the verge of apoplexy. Children who have never been to school recognize this figure. We cannot stress too strongly that parents teach best as parents! So do teachers, perhaps.

We must remember that young children's difficulties may well arise because they cannot perceive or perform as an adult. Shouting at a baby, who can only crawl or bottom-shuffle, to stand up and walk, may massage our egos but will only harm the child. Leave exhortation to the demagogues and shouting to the spectator sports. Children are keen to learn if we select the next step they can take from a firm base and if they know they can count on our support and encouragement. All learning is like learning to walk – it can only be done with the right neurological equipment and, no matter how eager one may be or how excellent one's models, a fear of falling can become a fear of failing. *Parents who keep before them the model of successful learning to walk or to talk will make fewer mistakes than if they attempt to apply someone else's principles of pedagogics or psychology. Progress in harmony with the child, confidence in one's expectations being realized, praise for what the child can do, encouragement for what the child is attempting to do and delight in who the child is, those are the really important principles parents practise so successfully.*

Who's for Teaching?

Millie has a PhD in linguistics but is currently working in a research team using heuristics to develop a multilanguage computerized dictionary; Fred has a small-holding, with a thousand free-range chickens, on which he and Millie live in Wiltshire with their 3-year-old daughter Kate. Who should teach Kate to read?

Barbara does out-work for a garment factory and lives with Lennie in two rooms in Tower Hamlets. Lennie is a lively 4-year-old. He goes to nursery school but still can't read.

Teresa and Mike have four children, Mary aged 12, John aged 9, and twins Patrick and Sean aged 2 years 9 months. Teresa and Mike both work in clerical jobs in Preston, a bus ride from the estate on which they live; Mike's mother, Maureen, minds the twins during the day; Mary takes them to and from grandma's on her way to school and back. Who should teach the twins to read?

With one family in eight a single-parent family, and one family in four living in poverty, below or on the margins of the Supplementary Benefit level in the UK, it would be fatuous to imagine that all families consisted of a working father, house-bound mother and 2.4

children. Today the question, 'Who should teach reading in the family?' may appear either complex or irrelevant. In fact, the answer in every case is that everyone in the family who can read can contribute to helping children learn to read, but the ideal person to make the major contribution is the member to whom children turn to ask questions, and the one to whom they run for comfort when they are hurt or in distress. If there is a choice, then the choice will be in favour of the one of whom they ask the most questions.

The person to teach reading is not necessarily the one with the most time. Nor need it be the parent or member of the family with the best academic abilities or qualifications. Millie, intellectually involved with her research, *may* find it more difficult to relate to Kate than her hard-working, chicken-raising husband. Barbara, home all day sewing, may be well placed to teach Lennie and welcome his companionship when he's home, after working off some of his energy at nursery. Should grandmother or big sister, perhaps, teach the twins or would they benefit most from closer contact with their parents, Teresa and Mike? If the twins are identical, wouldn't it be better to teach them separately, rather than together? To whom do they each relate?

Often the answer to the problems of busy parents, and particularly of single parents, is to suggest that someone else should teach the children to read – another member of the family or a friend, and failing them, someone from a voluntary organization. *We would much prefer to see help being given to free busy parents of some of their responsibilities or chores so that, if they are the ones to whom their children turn for help and support with their questions and their problems, they are the ones who can teach them to read.* Moreover, teaching our children to read in the ways we have suggested, is enjoyable, relaxing and rewarding. It should be fun and intellectually amusing, but never demanding. It should be in response to the child's interests and not something imposed.

Nor should teaching our children to read be seen as a form of self-assertion and self-realization, of showing the world what we can achieve through our children – that is no better than exploitation. Children are vulnerable, and parenting is responding to and meeting their needs, not using them for our own ends or as a means to work off our frustrations. Because parental roles have been so whittled away by the state, by the work ethic, the blandishments of consumerism, the pursuit of pleasure and the politics of sexism, it is not surprising that children today count for less. Divorce, illegitimacy, child abuse and neglect have all been increasing so rapidly in the last decade that, combined with the effects of poverty and unemployment and declining educational provision, emotional disorders 'may well turn into the crisis of our century', according to an officer of the British section of Save the Children. What is not yet fully appreciated is that these effects may be both cumulative and cyclic in their influence upon successive generations. In urging that parents teach their children to read we have no wish to add to this mountain of misery. We are convinced that a restoration of clear parental roles, greater responsibility of parents for their children, and an extension of parental involvement in the development of the communication skills of their children can enhance the children's emotional well being and stability. This, in turn, will develop more robust models of parenting, improve family life and ensure that future parents build upon firmer foundations.

The Barometer of Children's Behaviours

In deciding who teaches and how we teach our children to read there is only one barometer to watch – the happiness of our children. If the children enjoy learning to read and write, if they are looking around for more, if they come running with their books, we have made the right decisions. If this is not the case, then we must stop immediately and make a change. We can't trade in our children, but we can change the programme or whoever is doing the teaching.

When we worked with the parents of dyslexic and severely reading-retarded children, one of the most gratifying things to emerge was that the majority of parents soon reported a significant improvement in their relations with their children. They put this down to paired reading, but we were sure it was because they were helping their children to succeed and were praising them. Then some parents reported that their children were getting bored. When we investigaged the reasons for this we were surprised to find that the children were bored because they had achieved a faster rate of progress than we had anticipated. We accelerated progress by providing more difficult books and there was some improvement. The parents and their children told us subsequently that we should have accelerated this further than we had done. Again we had underestimated their potential. In other words, parental sensitivity was better than our professional tests and judgment. And parents don't wait for examination results at the end of the year. They are used to interacting quickly and intimately with their children. They are familiar with their children's changing feelings and behaviours. In teaching them to read, parents must continue to be sensitive to the barometer of their happiness and their eagerness to learn. The pace and variety of the programme, the degree of success the children feel they are enjoying, their relations with whoever is teaching them and factors within the children themselves – not least their physical health – must all be monitored. However, there is one problem which many parents of young children encounter. Some call it 'the battle of wills'.

The Self-Assertive Stage

It is a fiction that all children are lovely all the time, although we have been more frequently amazed at how sensible and resilient they can be under adverse circumstances, than at how horrible they can be. Parents who set clear standards of sensible behaviour and expect happy compliance rarely have difficulties. But even the sanest parents of the nicest children may encounter difficulties when, at some time in the first five or six years of infancy, children become self-assertive. It is usually at around 3 years of age that many children, who have previously been happy and amenable, may become difficult. It is quite common for 'No!' to be their first response to whatever is proposed, and for disobedience and obduracy to become almost norms of behaviour. Parents may need a strong sense of humour and may find their patience tried, especially if they are keen to start activities which they know, once begun, the children will enjoy. It is all very well knowing that the children are only exploring the limits of behaviour and testing how firm the ground is for manipulating their parents, a normal part of growing up, in fact. It is another matter to have to struggle with a child from whom one had become accustomed to expect unquestioning and willing compliance.

Children who have reached the stage at which they are conscious of their mobility and dexterity, who have been liberated from the tyranny of sphincter muscles and nappies, who eat virtually the same food as their parents, who understand almost all that they hear and can communicate their own wishes and thoughts, can be forgiven for believing that they have grown up and that all they need now do is assert themselves to get their own way. Parents, whose own development was arrested at this stage and are inclined to agree with them, will be given hell and may ultimately, after some years of attempting to placate and humour their offspring by buying their affection or cooperation, find themselves elbowed out of the nest. Rather than risk breaking the child's need for autonomy or his or her 'spirit', they break their own hearts and inflict another egotistical monster upon the world. Parents who assert their own authority, however, may find that they have a condition of permanent confrontation which they can only win by driving the child's need for self-assertion underground into areas, possibly outside the home, where they may not know what is going on until it is too late.

Fortunately, most parents strike a balance between these two extremes. It helps to be secure oneself and it helps if both parents agree on a common strategy. Children are born manipulators and some may engineer a split in order to play one parent off against the other. Consistency is vital. What helps most of all, whatever the circumstances, is to recognize from the outset that the child is going through a natural period of self-assertiveness, and that engaging in confrontation or surrender is therefore to lose. The answer is to ignore the negative responses – the 'No's and the refusals or disobedient behaviours – to change the subject quickly, and to take the initiative immediately by directing attention at something else.

We mention this self-assertive stage not because it is usually protracted or particularly difficult to deal with, but because the last thing parents want to happen is that reading becomes another bone of contention. If that happens, then there is no point in going ahead. Matters will get worse not better. Always start reading and writing sessions in a relaxed and cooperative atmosphere and in anticipation of fun and success. If self-assertiveness arises during the session, stop, ignore the interruption and count five. Then start again where you left off. No arguments. No confrontation. Just stop, and take five!

The other reason for looking closely at this problem is that it is common for children when they are tired, bored, below par, under stress and meeting difficulties, to revert to this behaviour even when they have outgrown it. Don't we all? Try to deal with such behaviour outside the reading and writing situation, again avoid making an issue of the behaviour, check that the child's basic needs have been met, and try to bring the session to an end on a positive note. Children are adept at developing a repertoire of task avoidance techniques. Usually prefaced by, 'I'm just . . .', they will announce that they need a drink, must go to the lavatory, can't find a shoe or have a pain in their hair. If we are not alert to children's real needs when they appear to be unnecessarily self-assertive, they may unconsciously learn a new task avoidance technique. Inexperienced teachers can be kept very busy while a class of children trot out their various individual diversionary ploys to avoid doing what is required of them. Once they find these task avoidance techniques work, like the rest of us, they tend to use them.

Checking the Balance

In starting out on helping our children we need to be alert to these pitfalls. Whilst reading may give great delight, children will experiment to see how it can be improved – perhaps with an icecream in one hand and a glass of coke in the other, one eye on the TV and the other out of the window. We need to check that our pace is right and that we have a variety of activities which will engage the full attention of the children. Instead of simply going on from day to day, make frequent and regular checks that everything is set fair for learning. This checklist will help to pinpoint possible areas in which the balance needs restoring.

FINE TUNING LEARNING CONDITIONS

* If basic needs for rest, food, etc. are interfering, get them sorted out first.
* Do you enjoy the sessions?
* Do you laugh and smile a lot?
* Is the child fully absorbed and involved?

* Do you talk and read in a warm and positive voice?
* Is the child talking tall?
* Are you providing for and rewarding success?
* Is the child over- or understimulated?
* Do you encourage questions and answer appropriate ones quickly, willingly and pleasantly?
* Do you ask questions the child can answer readily and correctly?
* Do you avoid asking questions which can be answered by 'Yes/No' and ask open questions requiring a more extended answer?
* Do you both work equally hard? Make sure the child has plenty to do.
* Is there plenty of variety of tasks?
* Do you stick to a routine that works – a set place, a set time or set rituals that help to get things started quickly?
* Is the pace keeping the child moving ahead with sufficient momentum so that the child feels progress is really being made?
* Are you satisfied that progress is being made and that the pace is causing neither boredom nor stress?
* Is the balance right? Is there a good balance between a variety of activities covering reading, writing and spelling with the main advance being in the enjoyment and understanding of what is being done?
* Are you using too many options?

If progress is being made and parents and children are happy one can have every confidence to continue. If this is not the case, try to put right whatever is upsetting the balance. If the foundations have been well laid in spoken language, then the children may be able to tell us, if we ask them, what they think is wrong. One aspect worth investigation is the possibility touched on in the last question of the 'fine tuning' checklist. Too many options, too wide a range of choice, breeds confusion. Young children, in particular, find it very hard to choose. When Winnie was asked, 'Which would you like, baked beans or fish-fingers?' the prompt answer was, 'Both, please!' Choice is a tyranny for young children and should be strictly limited.

Staying on Task, on Course

Teaching our children to read, write and spell arises out of teaching them to talk and to understand language. Throughout, we have emphasized the importance of talking through tasks as a means of learning to do them, and the importance of incidental learning around the home and in the environment. When children are involved in this dialogue with us, when language, learning and reading and its associated skills are all seen as real tasks which are thoroughly worthwhile, then morale is likely to be high. For this reason, if difficulties arise, they are best dealt with immediately and, so far as is possible, in the context in which they arise.

If a child asks for help or explanation in the kitchen or the garden, we try to give it there and then. If difficulties arise when reading or writing, that is where and when it is best to put them right. Similarly, if children get an insight into, or interest in some aspect of what they are doing, we are far better advised to deal with it there and then. Not only does this help us to keep everything related to the task in hand, it also enables us to deal with it 'on the wing', like all the other interactive incidental learning to which parents and children are accustomed. This is a considerable advantage over having to wait for other children's interests to be dealt with or for 'the proper lesson', as may well happen in school.

The corollary of this is, of course, that we need to be prepared with as wide a repertoire of games and activities as possible to use, on task, and to see reading as progressing simultaneously on all fronts, as language, reading, spelling and writing. We also need to be completely familiar with the sequence of progression in each of the main areas. Once a start has been made and paired reading, together with Language Experience and LE networking, has become well established, then free-range reading should be actively encouraged.

Free-range Reading

Reading, we have said, is a self-rewarding activity. So far, however, children who are only reading what they have written or what their parents have read to them, may not have discovered the delights of reading on their own. If they are going to learn to read by reading, then free-range reading is the next step. Just as they will have been reading in the home and the street, now we want them to be reading in comics, newspapers, magazines and books. It may well be that they do little more than look at pictures and advertisements in papers, or possibly check what is on TV, but they should be encouraged to do so. Comics, with their vivid graphics telling so much of the story, are ideal at this stage of supported reading. The cartoons, with the onomatopoeic words zooming and splatting between the bubbles of speech, help children to follow stories and to become familiar with the stereotypes of characters and the clichés of language. Parents, in our superior moments, may deplore some of these things, but we should have the humility to remember that beginning readers are meeting the clichés and many of the stereotypes for the first time. They will enjoy them as fresh and new – for all their possible banality.

Children's comics are their newspapers, magazines, journals and colour supplements and, whilst we will naturally ensure that they only enjoy the better, rather than the worse, manifestations of their genre, we urge that they are not banished entirely.

About books there can be no argument other than only the best are good enough, providing the best means the best children will read and enjoy. *A library and a librarian are a great help because there are so many wonderful books from which to choose. Some of the best are not even for reading, but are filled with pictures from the art galleries of the world. Some are full of jokes. Others tell profound tales in few words, tellingly. But children need to be exposed to them, to handle them, to know what is there but not have to read them all from cover to cover. Free-range reading is free, and the range limitless. If we are going to ensure that our children get hooked on books, we must let them explore for themselves under the guidance of those who know what is there.* Discovery may still be enjoyed, but exploration is quicker and more profitable because the course has been already mapped for us. We list in Appendix 9 some sources of books, but these cannot take the place of a good children's library with a librarian to point the way in uncharted waters.

At the same time as this free-range reading is familiarizing and exciting children with the possibilities and promise of reading, it is equally important to find books which they can read from cover to cover. They may well turn back first to some of the books, the picture story books, for example, we have read to them. Then we should be on the look out for simple, well told books in which pictures and text complement one another and in which those words which cannot be read can be guessed, or readily recognized once given to them. Start with the simplest and let the children feel their way. If the books are short and contain only a few lines of text on each page, it is always possible to go through them quickly, pointing out the names of the characters – these are usually the hardest words to read – and the more difficult words. This will normally be enough to start them off with a reasonable chance that they will get through to the end on their own. If they are successful, they may now be able to say, 'I enjoyed reading that!'

Free-range reading enables us to discover children's interests in reading. This may well be different from their other existing interests. It is a common fallacy that, because a child – or an adult, for that matter – is interested in something, they will be interested in reading about it. Sometimes, of course, this is perfectly true, but because one enjoys swimming it does not follow that one wants to read books about it. It is far better, therefore, to use books to stimulate interests and to discover what our children do enjoy reading. Again, like adults, children live vicariously through their reading and may well surprise us, even in this early stage, by selecting books which seem out of character. It was a surprise to their parents when the dyslexic children were able, for the first time in their lives, to borrow books from the library in the certain knowledge that they would be able to read them, to discover that many chose the Enid Blyton *Famous Five* story books they had missed out on.

Inevitably, in the pre-school and early school days, children will choose books that are too difficult for them. If they cannot be steered away from them, it will not hurt them to discover for themselves just how impenetrable books can be. A couple of experiences like that will be enough to encourage them to accept our advice. It is a good idea, if you find books which you are confident your children will be able to read and enjoy, to suggest that they may be too difficult or grown-up for them. This threat of banning will have the same effect as in the adult market, and be greeted with howls of protest and demands to read them immediately. However we encourage them, we want them to become hooked on books and to learn to read by enjoying what they read.

Check-out on the Programme

As parents, we get exasperated if we receive school reports which, whether or not they say nice or nasty things about our children, fail to tell us what and how well they have learned. We get just as annoyed in our work when we encounter people who are well qualified but not able. In checking programmes the important thing is finding out if our children *can*. Can they read on their own? What can they read? Can they write? Which letters, words, sentences? David Ausubel wrote:

> If I had to reduce all of educational psychology to just one principle I would say this: The most important single factor influencing learning is what the learner already knows. Ascertain this and teach accordingly.

Because parents know children so intimately, they teach them so well. Although in Appendix 8 we give some simple tests, these are but yardsticks or benchmarks along the road to literacy. Parents' own detailed knowledge of what their children can do is the best possible guide to how successfully the programme is working. Assuming that a start was made far enough back, at which point the child was secure and able to respond readily, and that the programme of shared and paired reading has been correctly and enjoyably introduced, it will help to check the following points before moving on to the next stage of prepared reading.

PROGRESS CHECKLIST

* Follows text as it is read in paired reading.
* Reads in unison/reads along.
* Supplies next word(s) in paired reading.
* Reads aloud alone in paired reading.
* Reads environmental print.
* Reads comics and looks at papers/magazines to read advertisements, captions and to find out sports results/TV programmes etc.
* Reads books of parent's choice in free time/in bed.
* Reads simple books of own choice for enjoyment.
* Writes own name in full.

* Writes words using letters of own name.
* Writes and spells correctly words taught so far.
* Writes and spells correctly sentences of news or picture titles.
* Writes and spells most words correctly in LE stories.
* Reads LE exchange if networking.
* Has announced, 'I can read'.
* Has announced, 'I liked reading that', or 'I enjoyed reading that' or something similar.
* Appears eager to read alone more widely books of greater difficulty.

In using the above checklist, remember that there is a difference between just being able to do something, doing it competently and doing it with mastery. Children are strongly motivated to achieve, and like to persist at tasks – like catching a ball – until they have mastered them. Once mastered, the tasks are automatized and performed without conscious effort. Ask yourself of a child's performance of a skill:

HOW FAR TO MASTERY AND AUTOMIZATION?

* Sometimes does it.
* Able to do it.
* Does it competently.
* Does it effortlessly.

Because children are strongly motivated to achieve, stay on each stage in the checklist until it is mastered. This does *not* mean that the next stage should not be introduced. It does mean that we should continue to provide opportunities for mastery on tasks until they have been accomplished successfully, even after we have moved on to higher steps in the sequence. Again, whilst it helps if reading and writing advance in parallel, they should not run in lock-step with one another. Move ahead in these areas independently, providing delay in one does not imperil progress in the other.

If it is felt that progress has not been as rapid or as smooth as anticipated, provide more exercise at whatever is the appropriate level. If children are enjoying what they are doing, that is a strong indication that they need to persist at it. Learning does not advance smoothly, but in a series of steps on some of which, as in normal physical development, some children stay longer than on others. Keep the enjoyment going, introduce games and activities appropriate to the level reached, and give diversionary activities which are enjoyable, such as verse learning or codes, or a complete break for a day or so. But don't be tempted to go beyond the child's limit of enjoyment and interest.

One advantage of working with our children in this language area is that their reading feeds their language development. They become less like the boy who complained, 'I see what I mean but I don't know how to say it!' Instead, they may become like Alice, who was rarely lost for words and demanded, 'How can I know what I think till I see what I say!' Reading and talking help us to enter into our children's feasible worlds. We increase the input of meaningful and significant language and they, in turn, are more able to express their thoughts and feelings. Many parents have told us that it is during these brief sessions of reading that they suddenly found themselves thinking of their children as people for the first time. One mother said, 'He was reading to me and it must have been the expression he put into it, but suddenly I realized until then I'd really only thought of him as a baby, an *it*. For the first time I saw him as a person!' If parenting were simply a matter of feeding children, cleaning them and keeping them warm, there would be a lot more abandoned babies. Because parenting involves cultural transmission, we find them interesting and growing into people, and hang on to them! If, ultimately, they are going to manage without us and enjoy interdependence, then in a literare world we must make them highly literate.

9

From Learning to Read
to Reading to Learn

When our children start reading books on their own, it is tempting to stop paired reading and to imagine that they will now move ahead at their own pace, or need no more help than being given a selection of books which get progressively more difficult. For some children, it is true, this is enough but they are as exceptional as those who discover how to read for themselves. Even the most able readers in these pre-school years will benefit from help. The vast majority of children at the beginning of reading not only need continued help and support, but may be seriously at risk, if left to their own devices, of becoming non-readers. Reading is the reduction of uncertainty. If beginning readers have the misfortune to struggle with a few books of which they cannot make sense, they may well decide that they do not know how to read after all and give up the unequal struggle.

We recall a 7-year-old reading a book which looked suitable enough, but which she was finding so confusing that she slammed it shut in disgust, exclaiming, 'I can't read!' It did not occur to her to say, 'I can't read *this*'. What she had been reading began something like this:

> Once there dwelt a Miller who bequeathed no more estate to the three children with whom his spouse had blessed their union but his mill, his ass and his cat. The partition was made without scrivener or attorney for fear they might consume his modest patrimony.

Not what Auntie had expected when she was seduced by the pictures of Puss in Boots! There's a world of difference between today's panto and Perrault's tale. But many children will be equally confused by the names of the vegetables encountered by Peter Rabbit in Mr MacGregor's garden. It is to avoid this possibility of confusion and disappointment that, as parents, we may mistakenly resort to picture books in which the pictures tell more of the story than the text, and that causes teachers to use primers or basal readers. In schools, as a result, some children take forever to learn to read.

There is no room for complacency about the picture revealed by Dr Barker Lunn, principal research officer at the National Foundation for Educational Research, of what goes on in the education of 9- to 11-year-olds in England. Based on a sample of 2500 classes in 732 schools, she found that, after arithmetic, the most frequent activity was silent reading as a class or in groups. Superficially, this attention to reading, combined with the evidence she found that 'the development of and practice in basic skills both of English and mathematics would seem to be the predominant features of junior school classrooms', might be reassuring. But when it is realized that in these schools only 15 per cent of the teachers regularly taught history and geography as separate subjects, 30 per cent teaching them as environmental studies, whilst 40 per cent taught science less than once a week, one wonders how much narrower education can be. What this means is that after four years of compulsory education, too many 9- to 11-year-olds are still plodding away at the pabulum of primers, vocabulary and spelling exercises, giving one word answers to comprehension exercises, or still learning their number bonds and tables when they aren't 'doing sums'. Many parents would be happy, of course, if they finished up at 11 years of age literate and numerate. It is time all parents demanded that basic numeracy and literacy are achieved by the majority of children by 7 or 8 years of age and that, thereafter, they are educated in mathematics, science, history, geography, literature and drama, music, art and crafts. And then, with increasing specialization in those subjects and in languages, in crafts, design and technology, and a range of other subjects, they would complete the secondary stage of education. It is a remarkable underestimation of our children's abilities if we seriously consider that they are only capable of a basic diet of the old three Rs until the age of 11, and not fit to begin learning about anything worthwhile until they enter secondary school.

As parents, we need, therefore, to ensure that children are saved the tedium of 'silent reading' in school and that they are able to learn by reading, that is, to learn by studying. To this end, we must make sure that the transition from paired reading is as smooth and as successful as possible.

Phasing Out Paired Reading

Once children consistently read aloud with confidence in the final stage of paired reading and are reading simple books on their own, we can begin to experiment by phasing out, successively, the early stages of paired reading. We can, for instance, omit reading the passage through and begin by reading together. Then, when that proves sufficient preparation, we can begin by reading together with pauses for the children to supply the next word or phrase. Many parents find that the children will take the initiative and indicate that they are eager to read on their own. Some children will say which stage they would like to be left out. What matters is that parents are there to supply the words which they may have difficulty with, and to explain anything they do not understand.

Phasing out paired reading like this may take a little or a long time depending on a number of factors. If the books are well within the children's understanding and are themselves strongly motivating – because the children are interested and want to know what happens next – they will help the children to remain print-borne. If the books are the ones which the children are eager to read but contain words and ideas they may find difficult then, clearly, it will take longer. Sometimes these are books they will want to return to again and again, in which case the second or third reading will be accomplished solo. But even when we have got the best match of books, some children will tackle them over-enthusiastically, stop talking tall and begin to stumble. Other children will be reluctant to start but, given help, will gather confidence and, with occasional reassurance, sail on. These differences within the child, such as impulsiveness, over-dependence, assertiveness, timidity, strong verbal memory, weak visual memory, nous, guts, brashness, or whatever traits may aid or impair their progress, are aspects with which parents are usually thoroughly familiar. We should use our encouragement and praise to help them to find a balance appropriate to the task. As parents, we must remember that to understand is not to condone. We may know what the difficulties are and why they arise but that does not mean that we condone them – we want them to go. Dealing with these minor problems as they arise in learning to read will help the children to overcome them in their everyday behaviour and in other subjects.

If we now only expect children to read to us books of increasing difficulty, we are rather like the parents who, having taught their child to ride a bike in the garden, expect him to go off on journeys of increasing length, and through traffic of increasing density, alone and unprotected. Just as we must protect and prepare the cyclist, we must protect and prepare the reader. Prepared reading does that.

Prepared Reading

Prepared reading means, first, selecting a book which is within our child's ability and which will be read with real enjoyment. We found that this often required careful selection from a wide range of books and here the public library is the greatest source of both advice and books. If one can come away with three or four books, then the final choice can be made at home. Having found the book which makes the best match, stick to it and don't worry if the other books are rejected. That is what libraries are for. Unfortunately, if one is dependent upon buying books then the range may be limited, save in the excellent specialist children's bookshops, and costs are such that few parents will want to discard books which are found to be too difficult. However, if books can be found that interest our children, that is the most important hurdle surmounted. Prepared reading may well surmount the other difficulties. If it doesn't, then recourse can be made to a return to paired reading.

Prepared reading requires the same preparation by the parents as paired reading. First, the parents familiarize themselves with the book, its characters, plot and with any aspects which may require some explanation. Having done this they can then introduce the book to the child. If the following sequence is followed, few difficulties are likely to arise.

PREPARED READING SEQUENCE

* Parent talks about the book, briefly outlining story and introducing characters; this can usually be done by reference to the pictures without spoiling the story.
* Parent reads from book to child for two or three minutes.
* Child reads the same passage silently, having been told to ask for any words which present difficulty.

* Child reads the same passage aloud to parent with such prompting or help as may be necessary.

Depending on the difficulty of the books and the children's abilities, the above sequence may be varied, either to include games, such as 'Find the word which means . . .' etc., or to omit the parent's reading. *As the aim of prepared reading is to help the child read with confidence, complete understanding and enjoyment, the one vital stage, which should never be omitted, is that in which the children read silently to themselves with the opportunity to ask for words and explanations should they need them.*

Usually, once parents are satisfied that their children are able to read books which have been begun with sessions of prepared reading, they encourage them to read them on their own. If this is done, then checks do need to be made from time to time and children should be encouraged to ask for help whenever they need it. If help is asked for, be as brief as possible, so that the child does not lose the thread of the sentence or story being read. It is always desirable to check that, before a child finishes a book at this stage, an opportunity is given for a passage to be read aloud *after* it has been read silently. The alternative is to ask children questions about the story to demonstrate how much they have understood of it. This, however, is a daunting task for adults and most children find it very difficult to retell a story unless they have the pictures, at least, to help them. Parents will find that a short conversation about the book will serve both as a check on children's understanding and as a way of making the passive vocabulary and language of the book active. Open-ended questions, such as, 'What did you like best . . .?', 'What did you think about . . .?' or 'Why do you think . . .?' are more likely to encourage children to talk than questions requiring only factual knowledge and one-word answers.

Again, armed with this information, parents are able to assess how progress is being made, whether easier, similar or harder books should next be used, and to identify any problems the children may be encountering. Some measures to deal with possible problems are discussed in the next chapter. If all progresses smoothly, children will be eager to read without interruption and prepared reading itself can then be phased out.

Phasing out prepared reading leads to guided reading in which the parents' contribution is concerned with pointing the children's reading in the right direction and monitoring, from time to time, the progress being made.

Guided Reading

Although children at this level will be able to read and understand public signs and notices and other kinds of environmental print, as well as newspaper items and books which interest them, they are still far from literate. Being literate entails being able to learn from books at a level commensurate with one's maturity and intellectual faculties. Guided and directed reading are essential stages through which parents can help children. The importance of these stages will be appreciated by parents who have attempted to help children with school projects, home assignments or homework: there often appears a great gulf between what children know and what books assume that they know. We also get insights into these problems when we help children to find things out in reference books and discover that frequently they do little more than add to their confusion.

Guided reading is not intended to restrict children's reading, but to extend and develop it. On the one hand we want our children to read widely, on the other we want them to read wisely. We also want them to be more independent in their reading without being insecure. As if these wishes were not difficult enough to realize – many of us wish that our children should not do as we did, but as we wish we had done! What we need to do is to stay close to our children and keep the channels of communication open so that they can talk to us without risking a lecture or diatribe. If we know what they are interested in and what their needs are, which are two very different things, we can strike a balance between them, and find a way through. This means that we also have to know what is available. *For guided reading is best described as finding books that will start to equip our children to develop what are called the higher-order reading skills.*

HIGHER-ORDER READING SKILLS DEVELOPED BY GUIDED READING

* Relevance of reading to child's own experience.
* Relevance of reading to child's own knowledge.
* Identifying the key characteristics/themes/subjects/ideas of what is read.
* Observing which events/incidents/statements illustrate the key characteristics/themes, etc.
* Distinguishing between kinds of reading – narrative, descriptive, factual, emotional, instructional, etc.
* Knowing what and when to skip, skim or concentrate upon when reading different types of material.
* Knowing how to find out: using the tools of reading.
* Talking about and summarizing what one has read.

Guided reading thus develops *the use of reading* and is concerned with preparing the reader before reading, and with the effects of what has been read upon the reader.

If we take a couple of books which parents might have selected, these bald statements will become clearer. One parent has decided, and we will assume correctly, that a suitable book to start his son, aged 7-plus years, reading longer and more demanding books is Roald Dahl's *Charlie and the Chocolate Factory*. He explains that the story is like the one about Aladdin, but in Dahl's book Charlie wins a competition and goes into a fantastic chocolate factory which makes things like lickable wallpaper and cavity-filling Caramels. 'The film was fantastic, too. In fact, it is an odd book for a Norwegian – yes, his name's Roald, not Ronald – who was an RAF fighter pilot to have written. It is punny, too, with square sweets that look round and characters with names like Veruca – that's right, you picked one up from the baths – Salt and Miss Beauregard. There are bits of verse scattered about, too, which can be missed out although they're amusing, especially about reading and Mike Teavee. But, when you've read it, let's see what you think about this sort of fantasy.'

Another parent, also correctly, let us assume, has decided that her 7-year-old daughter is so interested in science, and electrical things in particular, that she would get something of the feel of the excitement of science if she could read about Michael Faraday's life. She borrows a Ladybird book from the library because it seems the simplest account, although she is dismayed to find it is still rather difficult for a 7-year-old. 'This book doesn't explain the difference between batteries and generators you were asking about, but it does explain how it all began. It's about how Michael Faraday first found out that there was such a thing as electricity and went on to make coils and motors. Look, there's an inductance coil and there's a generator. No, he wasn't an engineer, more a chemist and a physicist. Like you, he wrote everything down that he found out and described exactly how he had done it. There wasn't much about electricity that he didn't look into, but I think you'll find that he did a lot of other things, too, like making stainless steel and the first heat-resistant glass. See if you can find out how he got to know so much over a hundred years ago.'

In both cases the parents are introducing the books in ways which will appeal to their children. Mentioning films and fighter pilot, or note making and questions about batteries were clearly intended to strike chords with the children. Whereas the father drew attention to characters and some aspects of the book, such as its humour and verse, it was the fantasy he was hoping the boy would enjoy. The mother, on the other hand, drew attention to the diagrams in the book and is clearly concerned that her daughter identifies Faraday's method of working whilst getting a glimpse, no matter how small at this early age, of someone at the frontiers of a new science.

Only when the parents have discussed with their children what they have found out or thought about their respective books will the process be complete. Before that happens both children may well have asked questions or made comments about their reading, the boy may have consulted a dictionary and the girl may have referred to her *Junior Pears Encyclopaedia* and tried some experiments from her Sara Stein *The Science Book*.

Just as parents help children to become conscious of the language they use and its appropriateness, or otherwise, to different situations, so we must help children to become conscious both of the language used in books and of the different ways in which language can be used in different kinds of books. The language of fantasy and of verbal play in the Dahl contrasts with the language of dictionaries and encyclopaedias. The descriptions of experiments, with their use of the passive, contrasts with the historical account of Faraday and the use of the perfect and pluperfect tenses. We use these grammatical terms, which need not bother the children, but the books use grammar and, by reading, children become familiar with it too.

Guided reading is built upon the children's previous concrete experience – in the girl's case with the 'experiments' she had been recording – and upon their experience of language in use, both conversationally and in reading. If we can relate these and bridge the gap to significant new reading experience then we are helping them to begin to learn from reading.

Parents will be helped in their own searches to find the books for their children by the guides to books listed in Appendix 9. It will also be clear from what we have said already that, if guided reading is to be successful, then children need access to a dictionary and information books in the home. Without breaking the bank or taking out a second mortgage in order to carpet the walls with morocco bindings, we do recommend that it is always better to buy the best reference books we can afford. In our experience in home, office and schools, this does not mean the most expensive and, in fact, paperback reference books stand up extremely well to hard use. But it does mean going for the best quality one can afford. Nothing is more annoying than having reference books which carry all the information you don't want and none that you do.

REFERENCE BOOKS EVERY HOME NEEDS

* The biggest Oxford, Chambers or Collins dictionary possible.
* A good encyclopaedia, say, Hutchinson's *New Twentieth Century Encyclopaedia*.
* A good world atlas.
* A good road atlas.
* *The Times Atlas of World History*.
* *AA/RAC Year Book*.
* *Whitaker's Almanack*.
* *The Guinness Book of Answers*.
* *The Guinness Book of Records*.

There are a number of children's encyclopaedias and dictionaries which are best chosen with the age and child in mind. Encyclopaedias arranged alphabetically, rather than in subject volumes, are preferable. Rather than a subject-organized encyclopaedia, we suggest buying good reference books on the subjects in which children are interested or in which we wish to interest them, whether these be trees, fossils, historical buildings or costumes, or games.

Using Books as Tools

Children need to be shown how to use reference books. Knowing the sequence of letters in the alphabet doesn't take them far in using a dictionary. Not only are some initial letters used more frequently than others, but dictionaries vary in the way in which words are entered. Some dictionaries, for instance, list each word separately, others list headwords and bury participles and derivatives beneath them. Children need to know how to use the pronunciation keys of dictionaries and to be warned against thinking that a word means only the first definition they come across. The example of how *we* use these reference and information books, including cookery books, medical dictionaries and maintenance manuals, will have a great influence on our children, and they will only begin to understand their organization through use. For this reason it is a good idea, when children ask a question we *are* able to answer, to refer them to the appropriate reference book and get them to look it up themselves. It is also an excellent practice to admit to the things we don't know and say we'll look them up. Children begin by assuming we know everything, even if they end up thinking we know nothing!

The fact they must learn above all others is that information is available and they can dig it out. The skill they must learn is how to get the information, how to assess the information and how to use it. For example, what is involved in finding out what and where to fish when on holiday in another part of the country, as compared with finding out about the ship in which Drake circumnavigated the world? Once one begins to get information on either of these subjects, some will be relevant, but most irrelevant, to our purpose. We may only want to know about fishing suitable for an 8-year-old, not about deep-sea fishing, and we don't want to know where or when Drake sailed but the name, dimensions, type and rigging of the *Golden Hind*. It is common in schools to find children copying slavishly from books when they have not even located the essential information for which they should be looking. *Going for the hard fact and reducing it to the bare minimum of words, organized in the form we want it, is a lesson children can learn at home.*

Using books as tools teaches skipping and skimming and focusing in on the facts we want. It develops efficient memorization because, having set out to seek something, we have pre-tagged it for recognition, reception and retention and, when we need it again, for retrieval. But, like reading, information retrieval is a skill that has to be learned by on-task involvement. There are some basic principles, and a paradox. The basic principle is to begin by asking ourselves what we know already about the possible answer. This is a vital first step because, if we don't ask ourselves that, we won't know where to look, we may not look widely enough and we may waste time scanning masses of information without being able to zoom in on the minute bit we want. So, in looking for the size of Drake's ship, we need to sort out what we know about him and ask ourselves some wh- questions about who he was, when he lived, what he did, where he went, etc. This will help us to decide how we might access him, and where. In a subject-organized children's encyclopaedia there may well be no entry under Drake, but there may be what we want under, say, Travel, Discovery, Exploration, Navigation, Ships, Tudors, Circumnavigation, Maritime History, etc. And we are looking for details which should include figures in feet or metres.

SEARCHING STRATEGIES – AND A PARADOX

* What's to be found out?
* What do I know already?
* Under how many possible heads?
* Is the goal general, specific, detailed, specialist?
* In what form do I want the answer?
* Decide where to look in order of the above priorities.
* Repeat entry name whilst seeking.
* Repeat goal whilst scanning.
* Continue search until all heads for entries have been scanned and information has been found.
* Check information is in form and detail required.
* Answer search question specifically.
* Paradox: what we find out on the way is often the most interesting!

Saying over and over whilst looking helps children to remember the purpose of the search. Determining early in our preparation for the search whether the information is general or specialist prevents us from looking in the wrong sort of book. Answering the question specifically at the end of the search makes sure that our mind is not cluttered up with a lot of unnecessary and irrelevant material.

We have stressed the use of books as tools not only because of its value and importance, but because it is something children enjoy doing. Children are questing and full of curiosity. In the days when schools wasted time and money testing what they called intelligence or mental ability, they would have been better employed estimating and developing the children's curiosity and showing them how to satisfy it. *Without curiosity, the urge to see under the stones and beyond the horizon, we are doomed to staying locked in complacency and obsolescence. Curiosity is the grain of sand beneath the shell of our skulls which forms the seed pearls of wisdom and knowledge. That is why setting children off on finding out information helps them to find what interests them on the way.* This is one of the advantages of also having around the house books that are treasuries which will feed their imaginations and their curiosity.

Books as Treasuries

At one time every cultured man would attempt to have a library of the most important books of his own and past ages. With the thousands of books which stream daily from the presses, this has long been unrealistic. Towns and cities have difficulty enough in having modest collections of significant books. Libraries cannot cope with the demands for books and we all have to limit the number of books we have the time to read. But there has grown up a kind of book which, whether as an anthology or treasury, attempts to collect together a lot in a little space.

If children are going to develop awareness of the diversity of language in print, they need books into which they can dip from time to time. Dipping when the time is ripe is more refreshing than cold and prolonged immersion.

The books we have in mind can, for the most part, be chosen from a wide selection. Most are in paperback and all are exceptionally cheap. Only the first needs a word of explanation. Brewer's *Dictionary of Phrase and Fable* is the sort of book that contains all the information you thought you would never want to know, or thought you knew already until you needed it. From 'Al at Lloyds' to 'Zoot suits', it is the most fascinating and seductive of reference books of Anglo-American words and phrases one could wish for.

TREASURIES TO TURN TO

* A book of jokes (Puffin, Ward Lock, etc.).
* A book of codes (for example, Puffin's *Codes for Kids*).
* A book of games (Hamlyn, Dent, etc.).
* A book of word games.
* A book of nonsense and comic verse.
* An anthology of poetry (for example, *This Way Delight* edited by Herbert Read, Faber).
* *Pears Junior Encyclopaedia* (excellent general information book).
* Brewer's *Dictionary of Phrase and Fable*.

Guided reading and the use of reference books, combined with the development of study habits, introduce children to studying and to using reading in order to learn. The extent to which this is done by parents is for them to decide. Our view is that, providing always they are guided by their children's interest and enjoyment, parents have a responsibility to stimulate curiosity, to motivate their children to explore and learn, and to encourage them to develop interests and hobbies which will make them active participants in finding out about their world, their society and their culture. Many of these interests may be sparked off by what they hear being talked about and discussed at home, at school and on television. In all cases we want them in the active apprenticeship role.

Directed Reading

The constant help and guidance that parents are able to bring to guided reading take on a new dimension in directed reading. *Directed reading focuses attention on key facts, concepts, ideas, on specialist or technical vocabulary and on the substance of the text being studied*. If guided reading is largely indicating to the reader where and what to read, directed reading is concerned with what the reader does when he arrives at the appropriate book or passage in the book. Directed reading is what teachers or lecturers should be about when they introduce a topic, illustrate and illuminate key concepts, themes, principles, ideas, facts or arguments, and then direct the students to text books or primary sources with instructions on what to look for and think about, examine, discuss, analyse or explore.

Directed reading is reading across the curriculum and is, therefore, different from general or free-range reading. Children who have been using books as tools will already have become familiar with many aspects of the techniques of skimming and skipping, and of thinking about and organizing what they have found. Directed reading takes everything a stage further into learning in a planned and organized manner. If it is seen as growing out of guided reading, then its main features extend from finding facts to going beyond the information given and the application of what has been learned. Directed reading is, therefore, the use of the higher-order reading skills to learning, studying and research. It is as appropriate to the child trying to find out how cosmetics are made as to the researcher seeking the latest papers on evidence of biochemical changes in synapses in the brain.

HIGHER-ORDER READING SKILLS INVOLVED IN LEARNING BY READING

* Reading for finding (facts, figures, info).
* Reading for following (story line, gist, argument).
* Reading for concepts (key ideas, opinions, principles).
* Reading for instruction (recipes, experiment, sequence of events).
* Reading for organization (relationships between facts and ideas).
* Reading for appreciation (identifying style, organization, values).
* Reading for appraisal (applying values and making criticism of what is read).
* Reading for inference (going beyond the information given, imagining, deducing, inferring, posing new problems, gaining new insights).
* Reading selectively, critically and reflectively using all the above.

Presented in an organized list such as this, the higher-order skills of reading appear more formidable than they really are. How many of us, after watching our team play rugby, football or cricket, do not apply all of the above criteria, and a lot of invective, too, when we read newspaper reports of the game? These criteria are precisely those we use when choosing and discussing the books we read, whether they be gardening manuals, whodunnits or on mathematical logic. They demonstrate that learning to read is not a one-off matter of getting the knack, but a process which requires continuous guidance, development and exercise. *We must learn that print has no authority or substance, and that what it means is usually in proportion to the knowledge and understanding we bring to it. The medium is not the message, but the meaning is.* Throughout their education, the partnership of parents and teachers can help our children learn to find the meaning behind the print and to learn from it. The importance of this partnership is highlighted by the inadequacies of text books and the difficulties many pupils and students experience in completing homework or assignments.

Learning from Text Books

Text books serve a valuable purpose in presenting, in sequential form, the knowledge of a subject considered appropriate to the levels of understanding of pupils in the process of learning it. Apart from their inbuild defects of being out of date, since knowledge, even our knowledge of the past, moves on and judgments of appropriateness and examiners' fashions change, the major deficiency of text books is that they are without feedback. If a lecturer or teacher begins by saying, 'In Apulia . . .', she will know from the expressions on her students' faces whether or not she can go on without an explanatory word or two. Not so the text book. No matter how carefully organized and how simply written, text books cannot meet all our needs and blind spots.

One of the major problems with school text books is that they have to be concise. Concision makes for heavy reading. Every word and phrase counts. Blink and you miss a century, as a historian remarked of one school history book. It was he who, on another occasion, looked in on a history lesson in one of our better independent schools and, noting that every pupil had his head in a text book, remarked to the master, 'May I compliment you on an excellent lesson – a reading lesson, I assume!' Text books are *not* meant to be read, of course. They are meant to be referred to and to be consulted. The good teacher tells pupils in advance what he or she will be discussing or examining, tells them what to look at in the text books they are using so that they will come prepared, and then explains, illustrates and demonstrates the main points of the subject. In the course of this, reference may or may not be made to the text book. Subsequently, however, the text book will be used to assist in the writing up of notes and the pupils will be told which parts of the text book to consult or study. They may well be told what to skip and what to concentrate upon, and advised on what use should be made of the text book in assignments or homework. In some instances pupils will be told what notes to make from their text books and how to make them. Today, increasingly, pupils should be encouraged to make models or diagrams to show the interrelated nature of events or processes.

Unfortunately, many teachers assume that all pupils have been instructed in how to study and how to use text books. They also often assume that all their pupils can read the text books and that, if they cannot, then it is someone else's job to teach them. It is far from uncommon to find that able mathematics and science pupils are held back by inadequate levels of reading and spelling. How much greater are the difficulties of pupils who have no specific bent for mathematics or the sciences and whose reading is inadequate for the understanding of the text books. The whole purpose of teachers is to engage pupils in dialogues which arise out of experiences they devise to illuminate and expound the disciplines they are trained to teach. Only through these dialogues can the pupils learn the vocabularies, concepts and principles which are particular to the disciplines. It helps if a child has seen a field, for example, to learn at school about an ice field. Without direct experience and explanation, the same child must be excused should she fail to understand a text book reference to a field in algebra, a field of force in physics and a fieldpiece in history.

Bridging the Mis-match Gap

With the exception of certain aspects of thinking in music, mathematics and art, all thought is dependent upon the organizing, classifying and amplifying use of language. Teaching areas of knowledge, disciplines or subjects demands that we familiarize pupils with key vocabulary, concepts, techniques and processes before they are exposed to the arid, condensed and constricted prose of text books. When, as parents, we become aware of difficulties our chil-

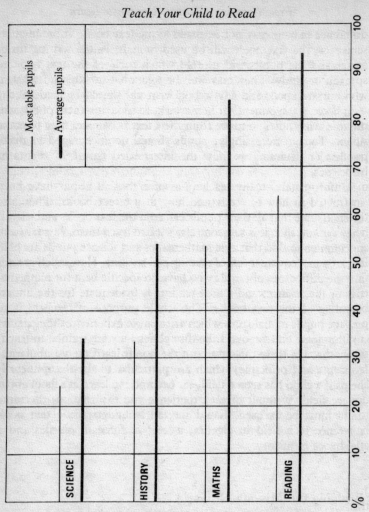

MATCHING WORK TO ABILITY

The graph shows the percentage of classes for which work in the subjects stated was satisfactorily matched to the pupils' abilities. For example, in science only 24 per cent of classes of the most able pupils were working at a sufficiently high level.

Statistics from 'Primary Education in England: a Survey by HM Inspectors of Schools', DES, HMSO, 1978. The report says that, 'In almost all the cases where work was not reasonably matched to children's capabilities, it was insufficiently demanding.'

dren may be having with homework or in keeping up in subjects at school, we will help them most if we try to put some blood and flesh around the bare bones of the text books. We don't need to be specialists ourselves, but if we have the humility to attempt to learn with our children we may be able to help when teachers have failed.

The fact is that there is often a considerable mis-match between pupils' ability, their reading ability and their attainments in various subject areas. This is shown in the diagram, which represents the position at primary level. Unless drastic action is taken, the gaps between potential and reading ability, on the one hand, and attainment in the various subjects, on the other, will increase with age.

When the parents involved in our action research project helped their children with severe reading difficulties with their school homework, they had a marked effect upon their children's performance. By reading over the questions and highlighting the nature of the information they were intended to elicit, they helped themselves and their children to focus upon what had to be found out. Then, by talking over with the children what was in their note books and text books, they were able to find the relevant passages. Using the prepared-reading technique, they then explained any difficulties or confusions in the passage and were able to help the children form their answers. Almost invariably, they found that their children had failed to understand a new term, a key concept or to relate what they already knew to new facts. Often, because the children had confidence in and respect for their parents who had helped them to learn to read, talking about their difficulties in these school subjects helped the children to solve their own problems with the minimum amount of prompting and explanation from the parents.

Parents who have forgotten, or never studied a particular subject at school or university, should not imagine that they cannot help. Judges daily decide on matters such as murder and arson which they themselves, it is assumed, have not experienced. Politicians daily decide upon matters of which they wot not. All of us daily use machines and substances we could neither make nor adequately describe. At the intellectual levels at which most of our children function, it is possible to explain everything they are required to know in simpler terms within the terms of the subject concerned. This is what Jerome Bruner means when he says that, 'any subject can be taught to any child in some honest form'. It is what William

Labov was asserting when he wrote that, 'an adult must enter into the right social relation with a child if he wants to find out what a child can do: this is just what many teachers cannot do'. It is just what parents can and do do so well.

Based on our experience with the parents' success in helping their children and on our subsequent experience, we have no hesitation in urging parents to encourage their children to discuss these and similar difficulties with them. The parents' knowledge of how their children think, of what they know already, their willingness to listen and to respect their children for what they are (whether or not they know the second law of thermodynamics or who saw Banquo's ghost), these are the qualities which will overcome these problems. Our humility in not knowing the answer and our willingness to try to find it will help enormously, too.

BRIDGING THE LEARNING MIS-MATCH GAP

* Does the child understand the question or problem?
* What parts of the question are known and which not known?
* What are the key facts, concepts, ideas, to be found out?
* At what point is the child absolutely secure and confident?
* What are the links between what the child knows thoroughly and what he needs to know?
* Can the question be answered or problem solved by a 'for instance' or analogy?
* Can the explanation be simplified by making a model, diagram, sketch, flow chart, map?
* Where in the child's notes or text book are the key facts, ideas, concepts, events?
* Are more facts or clearer explanations in simpler terms needed from other reference books?
* Having carried out the above:
    1. Go from the known to the unknown.
    2. Explain each step in terms of the previous steps.
    3. Use the simplest words, models, illustrations.
    4. Show where and how in notes and text book the facts and ideas are explained.
    5. Talk and read over the key passages in the chain.
    6. Get the child to ask the question in simple terms.

7. Get the child to answer the question in the terms of the text book and notes.
8. Get the child to answer in own simple terms.

So, a question about the local helm wind and zonda of Argentina leads us back to familiarity with seasonal winds. From seasonal winds as prevailing winds, we go to mountains in their way, forcing the winds to rise and causing the air to expand. Coming down the mountain, the wind warms and dries. Depending on the age of the child or on the text book, we may have to check out terms like pressure, precipitation, orographically induced winds, chinooks, Föhn or adiabatic, make a sketch of the Andes and Pennines, and see if the child can help out with a description of the helm cloud. In other words, it doesn't matter how complicated or difficult the physics or geography of all this may sound, nor how local its relevance, it does show two things. Any parent could have traced back the answer using the child's notes or text book, assuming they were available. Any parent who had worked his or her way through the steps in the previous checklist without success and come to the conclusion that explanation from another reference book was needed, would have found adequate answers in *Chambers' Dictionary*.

Reading to Learn

By learning to read by reading and becoming first print-borne, then book-hooked, our children become aware that they can experience vicariously through reading. They can experience the acts of heroism and derring-do, the fears and privations of their heroines and heroes. This experience of joy and terror, of distant places and times, as well as of people who are good, evil, kind, cruel, ordinary or strange, is a learning experience which can be more significant to them than events themselves, which may neither seize their imaginations nor impinge deeply upon their feelings. They may walk by a graveyard every day on their way to and from school but only experience horror when reading about Tom Sawyer's graveyard adventure. In the same way they may learn cognitively by reading. But just as stories must engage their imaginations and their feelings, so reading to learn must engage their intellects.

As much as we may use skipping and skimming when reading, reading to learn requires the identification of what we do not already know or understand and careful, detailed attention to the examples and expositions which explain it. It means finding the key facts or ideas and learning them. If we have been helping our children in the ways we have already described then they will have already experienced with us, the essence of what is involved. It is not just a question of going from the known to the unknown, but of first finding out what is unknown and then getting to know it. It is not just reading through to get the general drift or story line, but of re-reading to understand more fully and in greater depth; it is following the steps in a chain of events, argument or process. Definitions must be found, explanations followed, relationships established and questions asked and answered before we may claim that, in reading to learn, we have understood what has been read.

Learning to Decide

The way in which we described helping our children with their homework or assignments is, in fact, a way of introducing them to reading to learn. Reading to learn is studying. Studying a subject, whether plumbing at college or philosophy in prison, is the same as reading a subject at university. It is making a subject our own and ourselves a part of it. It is going from wanting to be able to learn a body of knowledge to being able to contribute to that body of knowledge. We need better philosophers and better plumbers as the quality of our lives and of our homes testifies. Arguments about instruction versus education are fatuous, as silly as taking a blowtorch to mend plastic pipes.

As parents, we can help our children to become educated by helping them to read subjects with understanding. Reading to learn and to use the tools of reading will take them beyond mere functional literacy. Functional literacy, no matter how it is defined, entails only the ability to cope and survive in a community or society. Functional literacy is dependence. The functionally literate are better off than the illiterate, who cannot cope to the maximum of their potential in a given society. But the functionally literate can be manipulated by those who print the messages. Full literacy means being able to contribute to and to decide upon the messages. It is not dependence but interdependence in a learning and literate community. In the words of Viktor Frankl, 'all education is education towards the ability to decide'. By helping our children now, we give them the freedom in the twenty-first century to decide for themselves.

Handwriting

The correct posture, a relaxed hold and saying the name and sound of the letters whilst making the correct sequence of strokes develop an efficient style.

Fading out and fading in again help children to end correctly:

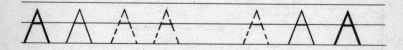

A First Writing Alphabet – the sequence of strokes:

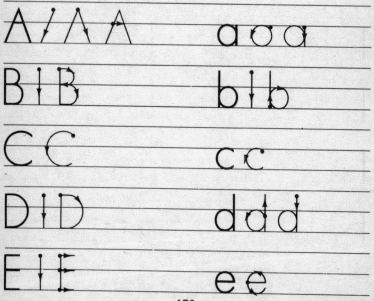

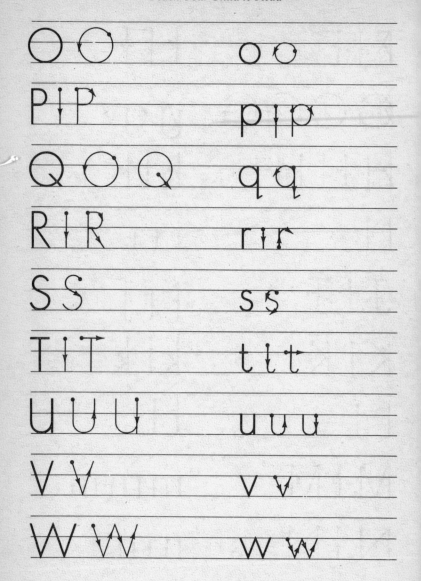

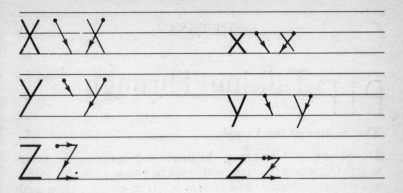

Talking Through

The Names of the Vowels

These examples of what many children say when writing their letters to help fix them in their minds need not be followed literally, as they will soon be discarded. Any form of words which helps them recall letter and shape in association with the short vowel sound and a word containing it may, of course, be used.

'A says *a* like an apple 𝑎 .'

'E says *e* like an egg 𝑒 .'

'I says *i* like an insect 𝑖 .'

'O says *o* like an orange 𝑜 .'

'U says *u* like an umbrella 𝑢 .'

Reversals – b and d

It is common for children to reverse letters and this should cause no concern unless it persists after about 7 or 8 years of age when it may be corrected, usually swiftly and completely, by the method described in Appendix 6.

The majority of children can be helped in the early stages of learning to write if they talk through the small *b* and *d* like this:

'B says *b*. First the bat ❘ and then the ball **b** .'

'D says *d*. First the drum ◯ and then the stick **d** .'

It is recommended that, should these 'talk throughs' be used, they be introduced well separated – say, two or three days apart.

Writing Their Names

The most important first mark they make upon their world is when children write their own names. First, the initial of the forename, then the name itself and later their full names.

James

Words made from the letters of James's name:

am as me jam sea

Alison

Words made from the letters of Alison's name:

is on no so sail nail

Cursive or Joined Writing

This simple cursive style is developed from the previous script. The same capital letters are retained and there is nothing to unlearn.

abcdefghijklm

nopqrstuvwxyz

(This style is used in *Write & Spell* by Joyce and Peter Young; Oliver and Boyd.)

James Alison

The ligatures or strokes joining letters are designed to enable children to write fluently and to develop their own style whilst learning to write and to spell.

Alison James

Onomatopoeic and Imitative Words

The only words that mean what they say.

Ah!
Atishoo!

Baa
babble
bellow
blip
bob
boo
boom
bray
bump
burble
buzz

Cackle
chatter
cheep
chink
chirp
chuckle
clang
clank
clink
cluck
coo
cough
crackle

crash
creak
croak
crow
crunch
cuckoo

Dap
dazzle
din
ding
dither
dizzy
doodle
doom
dribble
drizzle
dump

Echo
Eh!
explode

Fiddle-faddle
fizz
flap
flash
flick

flip
flit
flop
frizzle
fuss

Gabble
gag
gaggle
gasp
Gee!
ghastly
gibber
giggle
gloom
gobble
gong
grind
grizzle
groan
growl
grumble
grunt
gulp
gurgle
gush
guzzle

Ha!
hack
heckle
Hee-haw!
He-he!
Hi!
hiss
honk
hoot
howl
hubbub
hullabaloo
Hullo!
hum
humdrum

Jabber
jangle
jar
jeer
jink
jittery
jostle
judder
jumble

Knock

Lull
lullaby

Miaow
moan
mumble
munch
murmur
mutter

Nag

natter
neigh
nick

Oh!
ooze

Pat
peep
peewit
plod
plonk
plop
pooh-pooh
pop
prang
prattle
purr

Quack

Racket
rap
rat-a-tat
rattle
ring
rip
roar
rumble
rumpus

Scream
screech
Sh!
Shoo!
shriek
shrill
sigh
sizzle

slam
slop
slosh
smack
smash
sneeze
snooze
snort
sob
splash
spring
squash
squawk
squeal
squelch
stamp
swat
swish
swoop

Tap
thump
thunder
tick
ting
tinkle
toot
trample
trill
tut-tut
twang
tweet
twitter

Ugh!

Waddle
waggle
weep

whack	whoop	yell
wheeze	whoosh	yodel
whimper	wiggle	
whirl	wriggle	Zigzag
whirr		zing
whisk	Yah!	zip
whistle	yap	zizz
whizz	yawn	zoom

Write and Spell

Patterns of Writing, Patterns of Sounds

By teaching common combinations of letters and the sounds they make in common words, writing and spelling are taught hand in hand and both skills, with practice, become automatized.

The letters and letter strings are set out below, together with examples. They may be used, together with examples encountered in reading and Language Experience, both for writing practice and in the word games and activities.

Short vowels with hard consonants

am	an	at	as	add
egg	end	ever	even	every
if	it	is	in	ill
of	off	on	odd	ox
up	us	under	until	
bag	can	fat	gag	ham
bed	den	fed	get	hen
big	din	fit	gift	his
box	dog	fox	got	hop
but	cut	fun	gum	hug
jam	kangaroo	lap	man	nap
jet	kettle	leg	men	net
Jim	kit	lid	miss	nip
jot		lot	moss	nod
jug		lug	mud	nut
pal	quack	rag	sad	tag
pen	quest	red	set	ten
pig	quick	rip	sit	tip
pot		rod	sob	Tom
pup		rub	sun	tub

van	wag	exam	yap	
vest	web	except	yet	zebra
visit	wigwam	exit	yip	zigzag
volcano	wobble		yoghurt	
vulgar				

double vowels ee and oo

| bee | see | feet | heel | weed |
| too | boot | moon | hook | soon |

Ending with -ing

| king | ring | sing | wing | being |
| seeing | doing | ringing | weeding | looking |

th – 'the rude letters put their tongues out'

| the | this | that | thing | there |
| bath | moth | path | with | tooth |

sh – 'the quiet letters'

| ship | shop | shot | shut | shoot |

ch – 'the sneezing letters'

| chat | chop | chin | cheek | choose |
| much | such | rich | beech | which |

-all

| ball | call | fall | tall | wall |

Starting consonant strings

bl-
| blob | bled | bless | blot | bleed |

br-
| brim | broom | bring | breeze | brook |

cl-
| clap | class | club | cling | cloth |

cr-
crab	cram	crib	cross	creep

dr-
drag	dragon	drop	drum	dress

fl-
flag	flat	flop	fleet	flash

fr-
from	front	free	Fred	fresh

gl-
glad	glum	glass	glee	gloom

gr-
grab	Gran	grip	grub	grand

pl-
plod	plug	plum	plan	plop

sc-
scab	Scot	scoot	scooter

sk-
skid	skin	skip	skim

sl-
slam	slap	slip	sleep	sleet

sm-
smut	small	smash	smooth	Smith

sn-
snag	snap	snip	sneeze	snooze

sp-
spin	spot	speed	speech	spoon

st-
stag	stop	sting	stall	stool

sw-
swim	sweep	sweet	swoop	swing

tr-
trap	tram	trip	trot	tree

wh-
when	whip	what	which	wheel
where	why	who	whose	whole

Long vowels

a – as in April	able	radio	
e – as in me	we	even	
i – as in I	ice	island	
o – as in over	no	go	potato
u – as in use	unit	usual	

-ai and -ay – 'ai in the middle, ay at the end'

rain	tail	train	sail	chain
day	say	way	play	stay

ea – sounds like ee

sea	eat	meat	beach	leaf

ea – sounds like e

head	dead	tread	bread	breath

oa

oak	boat	soap	float	road

Final -y in three-letter words

why	cry	fly	try	shy
frying	trying	flying	crying	

Final -y after double letters

happy	jelly	silly	Billy	daddy
mummy	merry	fussy	puppy	hobby

-oi and -oy – 'oi in the middle, oy at the end'

oil	boil	coin	join	spoil
boy	joy	toy	cowboy	enjoy

-ou and -ow – 'you're stepping on my toe letters'

out	shout	about	cloud	mouth
owl	how	down	clown	crowd

Final -e – 'hops over the letter before to ask the vowel its name'

bite

hate	hope	tube	make	shine

Silent letters

b	lamb	dumb	climb	comb	thumb
g	gnome	gnaw	gnu	sign	foreign
h	hour	honest	ghost	rhyme	rhubarb
k	know	knee	knit	knife	knight
l	half	calf	talk	folk	palm
n	hymn	autumn	column	solemn	
w	write	wrist	wreck	wrong	wren

-ight

fight	sight	light	might	night
fright	bright	flight	knight	tonight

Vowels modified by a consonant

-ar

bar	card	farm	dark	arch

-are

bare	care	spare	share	beware

-air

air	hair	fair	chair	stairs

-er

her	sister	mother	father	brother
summer	winter	baker	supper	dinner

-ear

ear	fear	dear	spear	clear

-ear

bear	wear	pear	tear	

-eer

deer	steer	beer	cheer	

-ir

fir	bird	first	girl	birthday

-or

for	born	morning	horse	short

-ore

wore	tore	shore	store	score

-ur

fur	burn	hurt	church	purse

-aw

saw	paw	hawk	claw	drawer

-ew				
few	stew	newt	chew	crew
-ow				
low	show	grow	arrow	shadow
wor-				
work	worm	worth	word	world

Final consonant strings

-ck				
back	deck	sock	duck	clock
-tch				
hatch	catch	itch	fetch	Dutch
-ft				
raft	lift	soft	left	swift
-ll				
bell	hill	doll	skull	shell
-ld				
old	cold	held	gold	child
-lt				
belt	salt	pelt	bolt	spilt
-ly				
ugly	holy	badly	kindly	clearly
-mp				
imp	limp	romp	hump	chimp
-nd				
and	end	hand	pond	ground
-nk				
bank	sink	thank	blink	trunk
-nt				
ant	went	hint	tent	plant
-pt				
kept	wept	slept	swept	interrupt
-ss				
pass	hiss	fuss	glass	cross
-st				
fast	best	just	first	fastest
-sk				
ask	mask	desk	tusk	flask

Letters that change their sound

c				
city	cinema	circle	cycle	ice
g				
gentle	gipsy	giraffe	ginger	danger

More starters

dw-

dwell	dwelt	dwarf

ph-

phone	Philip	photograph	pheasant	physics

scr-

scrap	scrub	scratch	screw	scrabble

sch-

school	scheme	scholar	schooner

spl-

splash	split	splutter	splendid	splinter

spr-

spring	spray	sprinkle	spread	sprint

str-

strap	strip	street	stripe	straw

thr-

three	throat	throw	throne	thread

tw-

twin	twist	twice	twelve	twenty

qu-

queer	quiet	quick	queer	quarter

squ-

squeak	square	squeeze	squid	squirrel

sc-

scent	science	scene	scissors	muscle

Modified vowel sounds

au

Paul	sauce	haunt	cause	Santa Claus

ie

piece	field	chief	believe	shield

oe

toe	goes	heroes	tomatoes	potatoes

ue

blue	true	glue	rescue	avenue

ear

earth	early	earn	pearl	heard

-oor – makes two sounds

door	floor	indoors	poor	moor

-our

our	hour	sour	flour	scour

-our – as in four and colour

| your | court | pour | favour | harbour |

-ure – as in pure and fury

| cure | sure | fury | jury | plural |

-ture – as in nature

| picture | capture | fracture | mixture | temperature |

wa-

| wash | wand | want | watch | wander |

war-

| warm | ward | warble | reward | forward |

Endings and suffixes

-ed

| talked | pulled | called | brushed | marked |

-ed

| ended | mended | sprinted | shouted | landed |

-ied – 'when words end with y, change y to i and add ed'

| tried | cried | married | emptied | worried |

-able – 'when the word ends with e, drop the e then add able'

| lovable | likable | valuable |
| laughable | remarkable | eatable |

-ible

| possible | horrible | terrible | sensible | visible |

-al

| comical | usual | equal | medal | royal |

-el

| camel | tunnel | label | towel | model |

-il

| April | tonsil | pencil | until | devil |

-ful

| careful | helpful | cupful | awful | beautiful |

-le

| battle | little | apple | middle | cycle |

-ang

| bang | hang | sang |

-ung

| bung | hung | stung | rung | swung |

-ong

| song | strong | long | belong | wrong |

-ic

| comic | picnic | traffic | Atlantic | Arctic |

-age

| page | stage | cabbage | savage | bandage |

-dge

| dodge | bridge | ledge | hedge | ridge |

-ion

| million | region | fashion | onion | religion |

-sion

| division | pension | passion | mission | television |

-ily – 'when words end with y, change y to i and add ly'

| happily | daily | luckily | lazily | greedily |

-ness

| kindness | goodness | darkness | sadness | happiness |

-ought

| thought | ought | bought | fought | sought |

(But beware of drought)

-aught

| caught | taught | naughty | daughter | slaughter |

(But beware of laughter!)

-ough

rough	tough	enough
plough	bough	Slough
cough	trough	
though	although	

(But beware of through)

-ance

| dance | glance | chance | distance | entrance |

-ence

| fence | science | difference | commence |

-gue

| rogue | tongue | league | plague | fatigue |

-ology

| zoology | biology | geology | apology |

-ician

magician	musician	physician	politician	electrician

Common prefixes

be-
before	beside	between	because	behind

bi-
bicycle	biped	biceps

de-
demand	deserve	depart	delight	decay

dis-
dismay	distant	displease	dislodge	discover

ex-
expect	exist	exit	excite	examine

in-
inform	inside	include	invite	inhale

im-
improve	impact	imperfect	impatient	impress

mis-
mistake	mislead	misbelieve	mischief	mistrust

ob-
observe	obtain	object	oblige	obstruct

per-
perhaps	perform	perfume	permit	persist

pro-
provide	protect	project	proclaim	pronounce

pre-
pretend	prefer	prepare	prefect	present

re-
repair	refuse	remark	regard	reduce

super-
supervise	superior	superb	superstition

sub-
subtract	submit	subject	submarine	subway

trans-
transport	transplant	translate	transparent

un-
unlucky	unhappy	undo	unwind	unkind

Back Writing –
Away with Reversals

Children who learn to write in the ways we have described are unlikely to have persistent problems with getting letters the wrong way round. Should difficulties with *b, d* and *p, q* persist after 6 or 7 years of age, and children not respond to the technique we describe, then the following method should be tried. It can be used with any letters, of course, and may also help children who appear to have poor visual memories for spelling or who have poor hand-eye coordination.

* Stick a large sheet of paper on a smooth wall in such a position that the child may write upon it.
* Give the child a thick felt pen and position the child so that he or she can write with it, held at arm's length, on the sheet.
* With the child facing the paper, stand behind the child and with firm, steady pressure 'write' the letter on the child's back with the index finger.
* Check that the child felt the pressure and ask the child to name the letter.
* Tell the child to repeat what you say whilst writing the shape you make on her or his back.
* Say the name of the letter and the strokes you are making whilst 'writing' on the child's back, for example 'B says b, first down for the bat and round for the ball'.
* The child, using a full arm movement, reproduces the shape of the letter *b* in felt pen on the paper, whilst repeating with you, 'B says b, first down . . .' etc.

Over very many years we have not known this to fail. It is important to start with a large letter drawn with even pressure on the child's back and two or three trial runs may be necessary before the child is repeating the gross motor movement and the words simultaneously. Teach only one letter at a time. When all reversals have been dealt with, children may be helped to remember the spelling of words by having them written, a letter at a time, on their backs while they write them. After each session, they should practise writing the letter(s) whilst naming the strokes. They will now be using fine motor movements as compared with the gross, full arm movements and 'talking through' will help them with this.

Breathlessness, Stumbling and Pseudoalexia

Some children have no difficulty in learning to read but do have difficulty in reading aloud. Unlike children with speech impediments, defects or difficulties, whose difficulties may well be more pronounced when reading aloud, the children with whom we are concerned here present no difficulties in normal conversation. Parents should seek the advice of speech therapists about how to adapt the paired reading to meet their children's needs. Clearly, if children have impediments to reading aloud, then there are many ways by which we can satisfy ourselves that they have understood what we have read to them and understand what they have read to themselves – which is what reading is.

Children without speech difficulties who stumble, become breathless or 'fall over themselves' when trying to read aloud will normally be helped by paired reading. If this is not the case, then the following technique should be all that is necessary. We have used it successfully with severe and long-standing cases of otherwise able children who have failed to respond to a variety of therapies. Pseudoalexia is the medical term for the inability to read aloud and should be limited, like other medical terms such as alexia, dyslexia and dysgraphia, to medical use in cases for which there is hard medical evidence. All other cases should be described more explicitly and scientifically in English, for example 'has difficulty in reading aloud', 'is unable to read aloud', etc. Fortunately, pseudoalexia, beginning with the prefix *pseudo*, is not likely to become a popular subject for media attention.

* Select a book well within the reading ability of the child.
* Point to a sentence, ask the child to read it silently.
* Close or cover the book and ask the child to tell you what it said. Allow time between closing/covering the book before asking. Also, allow plenty of time for the child to answer.
* Accept reply with pleasure. In case of an unusually breathless or stumbling child, express pleasure at the clear unhurried speech.
* Repeat opening the book, pointing to a sentence, waiting for it to be read silently, closing/covering the book and asking the child to say what had been read. Say 'Good!' after each response.
* Gradually increase speed so that the interval between the child's reading the sentence and saying what was read is reduced.
* Eventually there should be no interval and the child will be reading a sentence and saying what was read simultaneously.
* After two or three successful, but possibly unremarked, readings by the child, congratulate the child on reading so well aloud.
* Repeat a further half-dozen times, reminding the child to read first and say afterwards, but without removing or covering the book.

In cases of breathlessness or stumbling, the child should be standing up and may, after three or four attempts, be entrusted with looking down to read and then looking up to say when instructed. The parent may then move further and further away so that the need to look up and to 'talk tall' is apparent to the child. The essence of the technique is simply to establish the habit of reading a sentence and then saying it, rather than having one function, looking, interfering with the other, saying, as was previously the case. Stress and anxiety, of course, should be avoided but the game-playing element of competitive fun will assist the process. Praise for clarity and fluency will, of course, also assist.

In cases of previous inability to read aloud, it is preferable to sit in front of the child – so that there is the need to look up to tell the parent what was read, but sufficiently near to the child to be able, at least initially, to open and close, uncover and cover the book. Once the read, look up, say pattern has been established, it may not be necessary to close or cover the book. With these children it is important to begin by asking them to *say* or to *tell* what they had read. When, eventually, they are told that they *read* something well, they invariably express surprise and delight.

Games and Activities to Develop Language

We are born with our senses but, without using them, we cannot learn to perceive with them. These activities develop perception, language and the faculties of our children – and are fun.

Hunt the Clock
Listening must be attentive. Hide a clock, later a watch, where it can only be found by listening. Cue the search by whispering 'Cold', 'Warm' and 'Hot'.

Hunt the Thimble
Hide a thimble or tiny object. Whisper instructions, such as 'Two steps forward. Turn left' etc.

Messenger
Instructions are hard to remember and harder to follow. When the child is not sure of their meaning, instructions are really taxing. Start simply and gradually build up to seven – plus or minus two – instructions. For example 'Put the letter/toy on the chair', leading to, ultimately, 'Walk backwards to the door, turn, open the door with your left hand, go to the kitchen, look in the third drawer . . .'

What Is It?
A mask or blindfold is used and the child sits facing away from the parent. If the object is not identified by one sense, use another and, if that fails, give verbal clues. Objective: to identify objects by their sound, touch, taste and smell.

Any everyday household objects, substances that are safe, may be used and each may be used for identification by different senses. The rustle of a newspaper, its feel or its smell, for example. Furniture may be identified by the noises it makes, the opening of a drawer, the sound of the rungs of a chair. Small pieces of bread, cornflake, cheese, soap, tea etc. may be used for smelling and/or tasting. Cutlery, crockery, fabrics etc. may be presented for identification through the least likely of the senses.

I Spy

Excellent for developing perception of letter sounds, so begin with the letter sounds rather than their names, and only gradually move on to the letter names. Move on, too, to the names of common things whose names are not so commonly used, such as skirting, architrave, screw-head, striker-plate, coving etc.

I Spy, if enjoyed, may be modified to '*I Hear* something beginning with . . .' which is most fun when played out-of-doors.

Naming the Parts

'He doesn't know his nose from his elbow!' and similar remarks highlight the importance of children knowing the names of the parts of their own bodies. 'Touch your . . .' is the command which can take children from knowing only hand and mouth to Achilles' tendon and umbilicus, etc. Important to play this before playing O'Grady.

To externalize this knowledge, draw round the child on to bits of card, cut out and join together at joints with paper-fasteners. Now take turns with the child to name the parts. Later, make cards on which the names are written, to be placed in position when named.

O'Grady Says

Played first as a straight instruction, for example 'O'Grady says touch your chin', it continues through actions of increasing complexity to the point at which only instructions preceded by O'Grady are to be carried out. After three mistakes, the roles are reversed.

Feelie-bag

Objects of different sizes but the same shapes, rough, smooth, soft, hard, etc. are put in a bag. The child is asked for, 'A short, thick pencil', 'A long, round, thin and rough piece of wood'. Toys of various sizes may be included. Beware of nails and screws or anything which can get caught up in other things and cause injury. Note, the aim of this game is that when it has been played a few times, the child can find things described only by, say, their colour or the sound they make. For example, 'Find me the blue crayon' which is identified as the short, thick crayon by touch. Take in turns.

Experiment with both hands separately. If child has difficulties with identification with one hand, not experienced when the other is used, talk the child through handling the objects while they are in view. For example, 'That's the rough, square piece of wood/tile' etc. while the child repeats the description and handles the characteristic components of the object. Follow this by using both hands simultaneously in the feelie-bag and getting the child to say the name or characteristics when in either hand.

Grandmother's Cat

First played in turn, with each player describing the cat with an adjective, or describer, beginning with the same letter (or sound initially), for example, 'My grandmother's cat is a *bad* cat', followed by, say, 'My grandmother's cat is a *big* cat'.

Later, a great way of extending memorizing abilities, the players have to remember and repeat all the adjectives before adding their own new one. For example, 'My grandmother's cat is a bad, big, blue, bushy, beautiful cat'. It may be varied with rhyming words, such as, 'a bad, sad, mad cat'.

Mime

'What am I doing?', 'Who am I?', 'Which book/song/film/programme?' These encourage observation, imitation, self- and other-awareness, guessing and imagination. Start with simple everyday actions, such as dressing, washing and go on to the more distant and abstract. Take turns. It may be developed until charades is played.

I'll Tell You a Tale

Each player, in turn, adds a phrase or sentence. 'Once upon a time, a beautiful prince/was hunting in the High Street/when his wig blew off/ . . .'! Serious or humorous, this will extend narrative power.

Variations include beginning a story which is completed by the child; saying what happened before the event described; changing the ending of a well known (to the child) story or incident.

How Did It Happen?

Cut out or draw a series of pictures showing the beginning, middle and end of a sequence of events. Placed before the child in random order, they are first arranged correctly by child who then describes what happened. Start with, say, a stick figure diving into a pool, swimming and climbing out in three separate pictures. Progress to suitable cut-up cartoon stories from comics etc. for more complex picture stories.

What Would Happen If . . .?

Cause and effect, everyday events, the unexpected and the bizarre are encompassed by this game. Progress from the simple and everyday to the more complex everyday and thence to the novel. Once the game is established, make the requirement that the players must say why one thing follows from another. This will involve the use of *because* and causality. The game may be developed to improve reasoning and planning skills.

For example, begin with starters such as, 'What would happen if I turned on the tap/trod on your toe/switched on the kettle . . .' and progress to '. . . if I was doing the washing/was getting ready to clean the car/if the fuse blew/if a window was broken'. Later progress to, '. . . if it only rained at night/if we were all only one centimetre tall/if dogs could talk', etc.

What Is It?

This is an extension of the Feelie-bag game and may be combined with riddles. The objective is to encourage descriptive language and imagination. In the early stages, the child will be happy with the skill of describing or of guessing what has been described. Later, the game may be developed into Animal, Vegetable or Mineral in which the object is to guess the item with the minimum number of clues and guesses.

Start, for example, with, 'What is it that's pointed, smooth, painted and printed on?' for a pencil which, if not guessed, the player might prompt by adding, 'and it's used for writing'.

Many of these games can be adapted to involve reading and writing. As described in Chapter 7, picture sequences, such as How Did It Happen?, are a natural starting point for writing stories.

Written language games and activities are listed in the next section.

Word and Writing Games

In addition to those games and activities explained in the book, there are a number of games which may be played to help children become familiar with the encoding and decoding skills. In particular, they will help children overcome any difficulties they may have with particular words encountered in their reading or writing.

Link Words
An introduction to crossword puzzles, the word concerned may be used simply as a starting point to link it with any other BAT words, with words concerned with the same subject, or clues may be given to all the words. The word concerned can be identified, if wished, by a clue about its position in the passage of text or of writing in which it occurs. For example, 'The word has seven letters, will be found on p. 17 of your story book and is ridden. Link it with these names of things which can also be ridden in: BALLOON, BOAT, CAR, LORRY, TAXI, TRAIN.'

```
            T A X I
            R
            A
            B I C Y C L E
B A L L O O N       O
            A       R
            T   C A R
                    R
                    Y
```

Blending Blends
An introduction to word jigsaw, below. This will help children to get the idea of saying the two sounds in a blend. Print the letters on a piece of card and cut in a double curve:

b ʃ l   t \ r   s ʃ tr

The child is shown a randomly displayed array of cards, told which to find and, with the first letter in the left hand and the other in the right, is then told to bring them together whilst saying what they say in a blend. Children are helped by the physical act of moving their hands together, to make the cards join up, whilst saying the sounds.

Word Jigsaw
Cards on which words are written and which have been cut up as above in their respective syllables have to be fitted together to form the required word. The word is then spoken, but children may well talk through, as they assemble the words and name the different syllables.

Care needs to be taken to cut words only into the syllables into which they fall in ordinary speech.

ANT and CAT Words
This may prepare the way for calligrams. It, too, helps with syllabification. A simple drawing of an ant or cat is substituted in the word:

🐜 IC   🐜 ARTIC   INF 🐜   ELEPH 🐜   PL 🐜   GI 🐜

🐱 CH   🐱 ARACT   🐱 APULT   🐱 ASTROPHE

🐱 ERPILLAR   🐱 TLE

Word Hunts – Jumbled Words
After hunting for words in their reading books, it is an easy matter to scramble the letters of families of words and have the child hunt for

them. For example, 'Hunt the animals in these jumbles: **lino**, **neh**, **gpi**, **woc**, **taog**, **giter**, **kentti**'. Jumbles may be made of furniture, fruit, tools, toys, trees, people, etc. By using categories, attention is drawn to the way in which language helps us to order our world. This, in turn, helps memorization by tagging words with their categories.

Odd Man Out

Once children begin to become aware of families of words, related because they are about the same kind of thing, they can play Odd Man Out. This can be played with cards from the Word store or by simply writing out the words. For example, 'Which is Odd Man Out: **Black**, **Green**, **Chain**, **Red**, **Yellow**, **Blue**?' Start with only three words and a very obvious odd one, and increase number and subtlety as children become more able. This is a good way to highlight a new word or one which has caused difficulty. From time to time ask why a certain 'wrong' word has been chosen – sometimes children begin by counting the lengths of the words, sometimes their reasons are quite logical: for instance, in our example it could be said that black isn't a colour.

What Goes With . . .?

Either from the Wordstore or in written or oral form, all the child has to do is to complete the pair of words, for example, 'What goes with night and . . ./ cup and . . ./ knife and . . .?' Again, this helps organize thinking. By making children alive to the pairs they know, they will be more aware of new associations when they hear or see them. Begin simply and graduate to the Gilbert and . . ., Sodom and . . .!

I'll Read That Again!

Reading aloud can go stale – liven it up by getting the children to read like their favourite comedian, someone with a foreign or strange accent, a station announcer, someone of the opposite sex, you, etc.

Reading like the vicar or a politician, singing and chanting can lead to reading with sound effects: 'Once upon a time (ding dong) by the sea (seagulls) lived King (anthem) . . .'

Make Up a Tongue-Twister

A way of making fun with words beginning with the same or similar letter strings is to encourage the children to try making up sentences containing them. For example, 'Strong string stretched straight stripped strutting strangers', or 'Twelve twinkling twins twirled and twisted to twenty twitching, twanging twiddlers'.

Memory Games

It is doubtful if our memories can be improved, but we can improve the registering, retention and recall of information by efficient memorization. Children have good memories but are not usually consciously aware of them until their attention is drawn to them. From 3 and 4 years of age onwards, the games we play with them help this process. Games such as Grandmother's Cat help children to remember chains of words. Memorizing verse, riddles and jokes develops the ability to retain and recall language. The biggest aids to memory are undoubtedly interest and motivation. In so far as games help to make children conscious memorizers who are highly interested and motivated to remember, they may serve a useful purpose – which is why they must be fun. Repeating the names of things, classifying them into groups, trying to visualize them, tagging them with other associations, such as rhythm or physical sensation, all help efficient memorization.

In all the following games, motivation can be increased by introducing an element of competition – 'How many can you remember?', 'You only have half a minute to look at them this time!' Similarly, the length of time before recall can be gradually increased from, say, immediately to one minute, two minutes, five minutes etc. A small reward may be given if things are remembered the next day or the next week.

Kim's Game: Memory for common objects on a tray – start with three or four and gradually increase the number and the diversity of range of objects, that is, add some unusual objects. The objects are covered with a cloth, revealed for half a minute and re-covered. What's the limit – seven, nine, twenty objects?

Can You Copy? With the child facing away from the 'tester', who taps three or four times in a rhythmical pattern, say, dah, dah, dit. The child must tap in the same rhythm. Knuckles, coins and pencils may be used initially for tapping but later introduce a variety of combinations of objects to develop more complex rhythmical patterns. Sequence from three or four taps to, say, nine taps in various patterns before going on to groups of patterns repeated with or without variations.

Copy Cat: Start with a simple outline of a cat's face which is shown briefly and which the child is then required to copy from memory. Gradually extend to the whole body, varying details, position etc. Once the game is established, introduce funny shapes, other animal outline shapes, geometrical shapes and letter shapes.

Missing Word: Start by showing child a sentence, later a passage, which is then covered. After a brief interval, the sentence or passage is shown with a word covered. The child has to recall the missing word. Use this as a starting point for a guessing game in which the child is asked to try to read a sentence and to guess the word which has been covered from the context. Extend to passages with missing words.

Stringing: Here the child is told to listen carefully and then, when asked, to try and repeat exactly what is said. Begin with, say, three family names or the names of three common toys. Gradually increase the number and the diversity of words to be recalled. Of course, it's easier to remember three or thirteen things all of the same family such as cutlery, crockery, parts of the body, and much harder to remember disparates such as penguin, whirlpool, coconut, valve etc. Gradually, having started with virtually no interval, increase the time between saying the list of things and asking for their repetition. Start by requiring repetition in the right order. After half a dozen lists, change to something completely different. Parents will find it is advisable to prepare their lists in advance. Strings of letters, strings of numbers may also be used. Use the strings to teach memory 'tricks', for instance, remembering pepper, arm, plank, eagle, red, Saturday is easy if you notice that the initial letters spell 'papers'. Again, all memorization is easier if the items are repeated immediately they are heard. The competitive element is introduced by saying, 'How many strings can you get right?' or 'How long a string can you remember?' Let them win by, for example, saying the letters of the alphabet or counting to twenty!

Answering Back: This is difficult – Stringing in reverse! Teil the child a list of things or numbers and then ask for them to be repeated in reverse order. For example, John, Mary, Anna is given and the child attempts to repeat back, Anna, Mary, John. Continue as above in Stringing. Note that time is needed if the child is to attempt the reversing process mentally before speaking, so don't rush. This encourages rehearsal. Teach the trick of tagging the things on to fingers before reversing so that they are read off the fingers. Note that speakers invariably have three points they want to make – easy for them and us to remember – but that more important things are coded in sevens: colours, days of the week. Try repeating the days of the week in alphabetical order – it is said to induce confusional amnesia. It is also proof of the economy of thought efficient memorization develops.

Criterion Reading Tests

Criteria for children's swimming abilities might be: plays happily in water; ducks under water; attempts two strokes; swims three strokes to side; swims ten strokes; swims one width, etc. No one would suggest that this told us which children would become Olympic swimmers, but it would be useful in establishing how far children had progressed. What is more, the criteria could be defined much more precisely and could become increasingly demanding. By reference to criteria such as these we have a much better picture of real performance than, for example, if we were told that a child had a Swimming Age of 7.6 years. If the average 7.6-year-old can't swim, we have been seriously misled. Schools have been misleading themselves for decades by working out Reading Ages which told them how children performed when compared with other children of the same age on out-dated tests of word recognition or sentence completion. The following tests have no such vain or scientific pretensions, but they do set out simple criteria which enable us to determine how far a child or adult has progressed in becoming literate. They ask, 'What have they read, what can they write?'

Letter Recognition

1. E T A O N R I S H D
   n i h e d a o t r s

A child who can name or sound all of these letters recognizes the ten most frequently recurring letters which make up about 75 per cent of all text. The top line in upper case is in order of frequency.

2. L F C M U G Y P W B V K X J Q Z
   u y w b l f j c x q g m p z v k

A child who can name or sound all of these letters, in addition to those in List 1, recognizes all the letters of the alphabet. The upper-case letters are in order of frequency.

Name Recognition

3. Recognizes first letter in upper case of own forename.
4. Recognizes own forename when clearly printed.
5. Writes own forename.
6. Writes words, and recognizes them elsewhere, made up of letters in own forename.
7. Recognizes own surname when clearly printed.
8. Writes own forename and surname.

Little or function Word Recognition

9. To in is it be as at so we he by or

A child who can read these twelve words here or in context can read the most frequently recurring two-letter words.

10. The and for are but not you all any can

A child who can read these ten words here or in context can read the most common three-letter words.

11. That with have this will your from they know want

A child who can read these here or in context can read the ten most common four-letter words.

Environmental Print

Children's safety, comfort and survival depend upon their ability to recognize these fifty words wherever they may see them. They are not arranged here in either order of importance or frequency as all must be known.

12.

Men	Women	Stop	Halt	Cross
Gas	Look	Wait	Right	Left
Fire	Exit	Alarm	Way in	Way out
Ladies	Danger	Poison	Toilets	Police
Warning	Entrance	Doctor	Surgery	Chemist
Keep out	Ambulance	Hospital	Telephone	Private
Gentlemen	Inflammable	Post Office	Electricity	Deep end
High voltage	Railway station		Guard dogs	Level-
	Public		patrol	crossing
	Conveniences			

It is suggested that parents add to this list any local signs which warn of hazards and which they consider vital for their children to recognize. For example, Quarry, Blasting in Progress, Armoured Vehicle Crossing, Disused Mine Shaft, etc.

13. Child recognizes own street/road name and name of village, town or district.
14. Child can write own name and address.

Word Recognition – Diagnostic Check

By means of the write-and-spell word lists in Appendix 5, parents can quickly establish children's decoding skills. When using the list for the first time, the child reads down the left-hand column until a mistake is made, then goes back to previous line and reads across the page. Continue until another mistake is made. This not only gives a quick guide to the letter strings with which children are familiar and to the words they are able to read if encountered in books, but it also indicates the level at about which write-and-spell activities may begin. Remember, children will read the words in context more easily than in this checklist, but they will not be able to write or spell them so readily.

Books Read Criteria

By establishing which books someone has read, we have a rough and ready means of estimating their level of literacy irrespective of age, abilities or opportunities. The book criteria below are each followed by brief examples or quotations as a further guide to what is intended. These criteria are particularly useful as they are readily understood by librarians, bookshops and other parents.

15. Has read simplest picture books or easiest primer or basal reader.

    H is for hat and hand.
    The dog ran. So did the man.

16. Has read picture story books in which pictures tell most of the tale.

    Meg went to the house. The hen was not there.

17. Has read simple story book with pictures complementing text.

    When Jack got to the farm, Mary was waiting with the horses. She looked cross and angry.

18. Has read simple story with illustrations.

    The sun was shining and Ben kicked his ball. He kicked it straight at the sun. All his friends cheered. Ben saw the ball go higher and higher. He knew he would never see his football again.

19. Has read story books with occasional illustrations.

    The giant had rings on his fingers but Kotan saw that his hands were dirty and that his golden jacket was badly torn. She felt almost sorry for him. Here was a giant who didn't know how to look after himself.

20. Able to read adventure story books such as *William, The Famous Five*.

    They dug all day for the treasure but by evening everyone was grumbling. They suspected, as the Four Friends had known from the beginning, that no chest of gold doubloons was buried there. The rock was solid.

21. Has read simple information and general interest books and is able to learn from them.

    In the sand, beneath the beech and birch trees, they could see where the badgers had been scraping away in search of food. Their sett, or burrow, could not be far away.

22. Has read books such as Rudyard Kipling's *The Jungle Book*.

> An Indian grazing-ground is all rocks and scrub and tussocks and little ravines, among which the herds scatter and disappear. The buffaloes generally keep to the pools and muddy places, where they lie wallowing or basking in the warm mud for hours.

23. Has read books such as Robert Louis Stevenson's *Treasure Island*.

> At the same moment, another pirate grasped Hunter's musket by the muzzle, wrenched it from his hands, plucked it through the loophole, and, with one stunning blow, laid the poor fellow senseless on the floor.

24. Has read books such as Lewis Carroll's *Alice's Adventures in Wonderland*.

> For a minute or two she stood looking at the house, and wondering what to do next, when suddenly a footman in livery came running out of the wood – (she considered him to be a footman because he was in livery: otherwise, judging by his face only, she would have called him a fish) – and rapped loudly at the door with his knuckles.

25. Has read books such as Mark Twain's *The Adventures of Tom Sawyer*.

> What a hero Tom was become now! He did not go skipping and prancing, but moved with a dignified swagger, as became a pirate who felt that the public eye was on him. And indeed it was; he tried not to seem to see the looks or hear the remarks as he passed along, but they were food and drink to him. Smaller boys than himself flocked at his heels, as proud to be seen with him and tolerated by him as if he had been the drummer at the head of a procession, or the elephant leading a menagerie into town.

26. Has read adult novels by, for instance, Charles Dickens, Jack London, Jules Verne, H. G. Wells, J. D. Salinger, George Orwell etc.

Reading to Learn

27. At any age, the criterion is that reading ability should not impair the ability to learn from required reading in text and source books across the curriculum in mathematics, general subjects, the sciences, literature, craft design and technology and the arts.

    Mis-match may be corrected by changing to easier books with the same content or appropriate prepared and guided reading on existing books.

Books as Tools

28. Uses dictionary to distinguish meanings and functions of words, for example, craft; discreet/discrete; meet/mete.
29. Uses Yellow Pages for, say, finding supplier of glass cut to size.
30. Uses encyclopaedia to find specific information, for example, date and place of trial of Joan of Arc.
31. Uses encyclopaedia to find differences between processes, for example, between colour-mixing in painting and on TV screen and the arithmetical terms used to describe them.
32. Uses reference books appropriately, as integral part of everyday life and of studies, to access information accurately and efficiently.

Writing and Spelling Skills for Learning

33. At any age the criterion is that writing speed and legibility, together with spelling, should not prevent expression of thoughts and the communication of what is known or intended in subjects across the curriculum. Note-taking and note-making skills should similarly be unimpeded by writing and spelling skills. Spelling may lag behind reading and word recognition in the early stages of learning to read but the gap should progressively narrow from 8 or 9 years of age onwards.

What Should They Read Next?

Having established roughly what a child has read already, it is not always easy to find another book at the same level. A quick and ready means of doing this is *The Five Finger Rule*. Having selected what the child thinks is suitable, ask for a page to be read aloud and count the errors or unread words. If there are five or more on the page, the book will only be read with great difficulty. Choose something easier – two or three errors or miscues per page are unlikely to seriously impair understanding, providing the reader uses the context to guess and is prepared to ask for help from time to time.

Books about Children's Books

The Good Book Guide to Children's Books, ed. Bing Taylor and Peter Braithwaite, Penguin (new edition), 1984.
    Outstanding value, recommends 500 books, half in paperback, for children aged 0 to 12-plus. Authoritative and practical.
Learning to Read by Margaret Meek, Bodley Head, 1982.
    An excellent guide to books, organized in ages from under 5 to adolescence, with detailed book lists, and ideal for guidance on helping to get children book-hooked and literate.

Children's Book Lists

Write asking for these, enclosing a stamped, addressed *label*, to:

The National Book League
45 East Hill
London
SW18 2QZ

The School Library Association
Victoria House
29–31 George Street
Oxford
OX1 2AY

Educational Toys – Letter Shapes Etc. for Early Learning

Apart from Mothercare, W. H. Smiths and larger bookshops and stationers, many toy shops now carry a wide range of materials for early learning.

The Yellow Pages list the excellent Early Learning Centres under Toy and Game Shops.

Look out for suitable learning apparatus made by Galt, LDA, E. J. Arnold and other 'educational suppliers'.

Computers and Software

Since our early involvement in the CET National Development Programme for Computer Assisted Learning, we have watched the valuable use of micros in helping to meet children's special educational needs. We are in no doubt about the power of computers and the importance of children having early hands-on experience of using them. But we have been disappointed in both the theoretical basis and practical applications of much of the software for language development and literacy. Before being swayed by the advertisements and undertaking considerable expenditure on hard- or software, parents should ask what it can do which cannot be better done with paper, pencil, books and high-touch, user-friendly parents! Once literate and numerate, our children can begin to exploit the computer's potential to the full.

Further Reading

BOWER, T. (1977), *The Perceptual World of the Child*. London: Fontana/Open Books.

BRUNER, J. S. (1971), *The Relevance of Education*. London: George Allen and Unwin.

GARVEY, C. (1982), *Play*. London: Fontana/Open Books. (1984), *Children's Talk*. London: Fontana/Open Books.

KAYE, K. (1984), *The Mental and Social Life of Babies: How parents create persons*. London: Methuen University Paperback.

SMITH, F. (1978), *Reading*. Cambridge: Cambridge University Press.

TIZARD, B. and HUGHES, M. (1984), *Young Children Learning: Talking and Thinking at Home and at School*. London: Fontana.

YOUNG, P. and TYRE, C. (1983), *Dyslexia or Illiteracy? Realizing the Right to Read*. Milton Keynes: Open University Press.

Index

Index

Fontana Paperbacks: Non-fiction

Fontana is a leading paperback publisher of non-fiction, both popular and academic. Below are some recent titles.

- ☐ CAPITALISM SINCE WORLD WAR II Philip Armstrong, Andrew Glyn and John Harrison £4.95
- ☐ ARISTOCRATS Robert Lacey £3.95
- ☐ PECULIAR PEOPLE Patrick Donovan £1.75
- ☐ A JOURNEY IN LADAKH Andrew Harvey £2.50
- ☐ ON THE PERIMETER Caroline Blackwood £1.95
- ☐ YOUNG CHILDREN LEARNING Barbara Tizard and Martin Hughes £2.95
- ☐ THE TRANQUILLIZER TRAP Joy Melville £1.95
- ☐ LIVING IN OVERDRIVE Clive Wood £2.50
- ☐ MIND AND MEDIA Patricia Marks Greenfield £2.50
- ☐ BETTER PROGRAMMING FOR YOUR COMMODORE 64 Henry Mullish and Dov Kruger £3.95
- ☐ NEW ADVENTURE SYSTEMS FOR THE SPECTRUM S. Robert Speel £3.95
- ☐ POLICEMAN'S PRELUDE Harry Cole £1.50
- ☐ SAS: THE JUNGLE FRONTIER Peter Dickens £2.50
- ☐ HOW TO WATCH CRICKET John Arlott £1.95
- ☐ SBS: THE INVISIBLE RAIDERS James Ladd £1.95
- ☐ THE NEW SOCIOLOGY OF MODERN BRITAIN Eric Butterworth and David Weir (eds.) £2.50
- ☐ BENNY John Burrowes £1.95
- ☐ ADORNO Martin Jay £2.50
- ☐ STRATEGY AND DIPLOMACY Paul Kennedy £3.95
- ☐ BEDSIDE SNOOKER Ray Reardon £2.95

You can buy Fontana paperbacks at your local bookshop or newsagent. Or you can order them from Fontana Paperbacks, Cash Sales Department, Box 29, Douglas, Isle of Man. Please send a cheque, postal or money order (not currency) worth the purchase price plus 15p per book for postage (maximum postage required is £3).

NAME (Block letters) _____

ADDRESS _____

_____

While every effort is made to keep prices low, it is sometimes necessary to increase prices at short notice. Fontana Paperbacks reserve the right to show new retail prices on covers which may differ from those previously advertised in the text or elsewhere.